Rapid Software Development
with Smalltalk

ADVANCES IN OBJECT TECHNOLOGY SERIES

Dr. Richard S. Wiener
Series Editor

Editor
Journal of Object-Oriented Programming
Report on Object Analysis and Design
SIGS Publications, Inc.
New York, New York

and

Department of Computer Science
University of Colorado
Colorado Springs, Colorado

Additional Volumes in Preparation

Rapid Software Development
with Smalltalk

Mark Lorenz

Hatteras Software, Inc.
Cary, North Carolina

New York

Library of Congress Cataloging-in-Publication Data

Lorenz, Mark
     Rapid software development with smalltalk / Mark Lorenz.
         p. cm. -- (Advances in object technology ; 7)
     Includes bibliographical references and index.
     ISBN 1-884842-12-7 (pbk.)
     1. Object-oriented programming (Computer science) 2. Smalltalk
     (Computer program language) 3. Computer software--Development.
     I. Title.
     II. Series.
     QA76.64.L675 1995
     005.1'2--dc20   95-16527
                                                     CIP

PUBLISHED BY
SIGS Books
71 W. 23rd Street, Third Floor
New York, New York 10010

Copyright © 1995 by SIGS Books. All rights reserved.

HOMSuite and OOMetric are trademarks of Hatteras Software, Inc.
Smalltalk/V is a trademark of Digitalk, Inc.
OS/2 is a trademark of International Business Machines Corporation.
Profile/V is a trademark of First Class Software.
WindowBuilder is a trademark of ObjectShare, Inc.
Envy is a trademark of Object Technology International.
Other product names mentioned throughout the book may be trademarks of
their respective companies.

SIGS Books ISBN 1–884842–12-7
Prentice Hall ISBN 0-13-449737-6

Printed in the United States of America
99 98 97 96   10 9 8 7 6 5 4 3 2

To Mom, who doesn't know a thing about software ...
but knows a whole lot about being a mother.

About the Author

Mark Lorenz is a recognized leader in the object-oriented software industry. He is founder and president of Hatteras Software, Inc., Cary, North Carolina, a company that specializes in helping others to develop object technology successfully. Lorenz has over 16 years of experience working as a consultant to Fortune 500 companies. His extensive experience modeling businesses, applying methodologies, advising management, and utilizing object technology has resulted in scores of successful software projects. Prior to founding Hatteras Software, Lorenz was technical lead of IBM's Object-Oriented Technology Center. The multiple projects that Lorenz has been involved with since 1987 have produced object-oriented products in domains such as telephony, retail, banking, manufacturing, and insurance. Included among these products are IBM's StorePlace™ and Hatteras Software's OOMetric.™

Lorenz is the author of *Object-Oriented Software Development: A Practical Guide* (Prentice Hall, 1993) and *Object-Oriented Software Metrics* (Prentice Hall, 1994). He has published articles in *American Programmer* and the *Journal of Object-Oriented Programming*, and his "Project Practicalities" column appears in *The Smalltalk Report* (SIGS Publications). Lorenz has participated in panels, tutorials, and workshops at Object-

World, OOPSLA, and Smalltalk Solutions conferences. He has a number of patents pending in the areas of object technology and graphical user interfaces.

Foreword

THE THING I like best about being the father of four children is that now when something happens, I don't get too excited when I don't need to. With the first child, my reaction was, "Arrgghh! My child is dying!" Now I say, "Oh—croup. Better get the steam going." On the flip side, I don't say, "I want to give my child every possible choice." I now know that managing the choices a child is given is extremely important to their happiness and to their relationship with me.

Early in my programming career, I had the great good fortune to program for two years with Ward Cunningham. I've never met anybody with his talent for asking the right questions first. Sometimes it took a lot of guts on my part to follow him into uncharted territory, but he has an uncanny knack for knowing which issues can safely be ignored.

Back in the olden days (when we powered our computers with coal that we had to dig out of the mountains in the freezing cold), Smalltalk programmers were a lunatic fringe. They were willing to do anything necessary to learn all the details of the underlying system. They were willing to put up with arbitrary amounts of garbage, all for the honor of programming in Smalltalk.

Smalltalk development is moving into the mainstream. That means regular working programmers with regular working tolerance for garbage trying to use Smalltalk to solve tough but workaday problems. Smalltalk is evolving to meet their needs with visual programming tools, automated database interfaces, and team programming tools.

Smalltalk project management has to evolve, too. In my consulting practice (did I mention I was a consultant?), I see two project management failure modes. The two fatal assumptions are "everything's the same" and "everything's different."

The current status quo includes the belief that Smalltalk development is just like mainframe development, only funner. Trees are killed, documents are stacked, phases are shifted between, and all the good stuff about Smalltalk is lost. All the spark, the flexibility, the sideways thinking that makes a Smalltalk program qualitatively different are gone, vanished under a pile of specs and method comments and release cycles.

The freshman dorm, on the other hand, sees managers, programmers, and customers throwing off the shackles of conventional development entirely. Managers figure, "Hey, this is Smalltalk. My developers can do miracles. Its easier to say "yes" to customers than "no." Programmers figure, "Hey, this is Smalltalk. I can do miracles. Whatever." Customers figure, "Hey, I don't know what it is, but I like being told everything is possible. I'm not sure why the thing isn't finished, though, since it looked done four months ago." All this works fine until the project comes crashing to a halt under its own weight.

Some things about Smalltalk development are the same as any other kind of development. Without communication (programmers, managers, and clients all on the same page), development fails. Without rigorous testing, development fails. Without some fixed resources (time to market and to budget; machine resources), development fails. These are universal truths of software development. Programming 10 times faster doesn't change them.

Some things about Smalltalk are very different. We all grew up in an era when changing code was expensive. "Fixing a bug in maintenance is orders of magnitude more expensive than fixing it in analysis" was ground into my head. This assumption permeates the conventional wisdom of managing software development. It simply isn't true with Smalltalk. Changing a disciplined

Smalltalk development actually gets easier as time goes on. The more insight you record in the form of objects, the more leverage you gain.

This book is about navigating between the quick-setting concrete of Status Quo development and the degenerative chaos of the Freshman Dorm. It will give you permission to worry about the right things at the right time and still satisfy your clients that their money is being spent wisely. Your investment in Smalltalk will be safeguarded by following the advice in this book about what risks to take, how to manage the risks, and how to help your team be as productive as possible in the meantime. Mark's years of Smalltalk experience show through in the big bag of practical, detailed suggestions he offers here.

—Kent Beck

Preface

THIS BOOK GUIDES the reader through elements that lead to quicker development of high-quality object-oriented software systems. There is a major emphasis on architecting a system to make sure you achieve the benefits of O-O, reuse from design patterns through factoring responsibilities, project issues, and detailed tips and techniques for immediate use.

As do my other books, this book takes a pragmatic approach based on experiences on commercial object-oriented (O-O) projects over the last number of years. As such, it is intended to be used by managers, technical leads, and developers that are currently tackling the challenges of using object technology, iterative processes, and new team structures to deliver software products to the marketplace. It is assumed that the reader has an understanding of the basic concepts of object technology, including classes, instances, methods, encapsulation, inheritance, and polymorphism. It is helpful if the reader has a general understanding of O-O methodologies such as Responsibility Driven Design (RDD), ObjectOry, and OMT.

It is my intention to cover as many generally-applicable topics. However, since the language examples are in Smalltalk and some of the topics only apply to Smalltalk or Smalltalk tools, developers using Smalltalk will benefit from more of the topics than will someone using another language.

I welcome questions, comments, rebuttals, and other communications regarding the book:

> Mark Lorenz
> Hatteras Software, Inc.
> 2000 Regency Parkway, Suite 230
> Cary, NC 27511
> (919) 319-3816 (voice) / (919) 319-3877 (fax)
> mark@hatteras.com

Callouts

Along the left side of the pages of this book are callouts. Callouts are used to provide summarized text to enhance skimming sections as well as emphasis for key points. In addition, whenever you see a 🖝 , an item of interest is being highlighted for extra emphasis.

Terms

A glossary is included at the back of the book containing definitions for many of the terms used in this book. I have tried to be crisp in defining the terms and where I used them throughout the book. Hopefully I have achieved my goal.

Notation

The notation used in this book is from my favorite methodology (which is sometimes called OOSD) from my book entitled "Object-Oriented Software Development." It is a mixture of RDD (Wirfs-Brock), OMT (Rumbaugh), and OOSE (Jacobson). Use this legend for the diagrams in this book. (See figure on following page.)

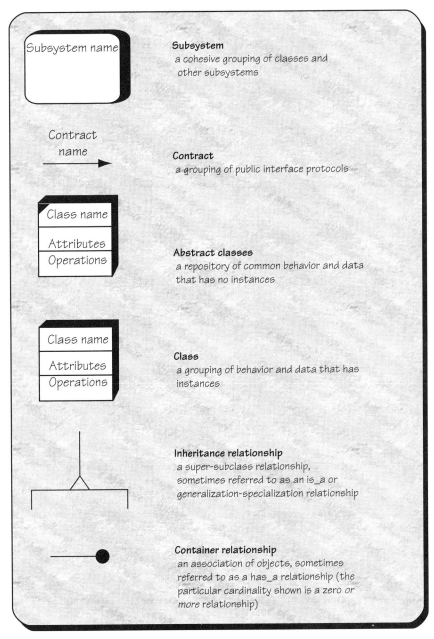

Subsystem
a cohesive grouping of classes and other subsystems

Contract
a grouping of public interface protocols

Abstract classes
a repository of common behavior and data that has no instances

Class
a grouping of behavior and data that has instances

Inheritance relationship
a super-subclass relationship, sometimes referred to as an is_a or generalization-specialization relationship

Container relationship
an association of objects, sometimes referred to as a has_a relationship (the particular cardinality shown is a zero or more relationship)

OOSD notation legend.

Acknowledgments

I WOULD LIKE TO thank all those wonderful O-O people that I have had the privilege of working with over the years. I would especially like to thank my compatriots at Hatteras Software, who gave advice and encouragement in this effort. Specifically, I'd like to recognize Bob Brodd, Bob Jensen, Denise Lorenz, Ted Eiles, Wayne Staats, Lori Wynkoop, Mark Wynkoop, and Peggy Hood.

I'd also like to thank my publisher, who did an excellent job working as a team on everything from the cover to the callouts (and no penguins!).

Finally, thanks a third time around to my family and friends, who put up with a workaholic's obsession with writing books, even if it kills me. Thanks for the continuing support. Special thanks to my mom, Iris Laverne Lorenz … I miss you.

Introduction

Now here, you see, it takes all the running
you can do, to keep in the same place.
If you want to get somewhere else,
you must run at least twice as fast as that!

—Lewis Carroll, *Through the Looking Glass*

CHANGES in the world are occurring in an ever-increasing rate. Computers are being used to keep up with these changes as never before. More and more American households have a personal computer. At the same time, student enrollment in computer science programs in our universities is declining at an alarming rate.

So, how are we to keep up? Computer hardware has seen rapid declines in costs while increasing capabilities at the same time. How has this been possible? One of the primary reasons this is happening is reuse of off-the-shelf componentry. Historically, we have not been able to achieve the same productivity in software development.

One technological trend that can help is object-oriented technology. The principles underlying this new way of developing software allow software systems to be developed faster and cheaper than ever before. The computer industry is investing heavily in this technology, with revenues from products using object technology more than tripling in the next 4 years. However, object technology is not a panacea. It involves an investment, which like all investments pays dividends over time. The big long-term paybacks are in increased reuse of software components and reduced maintenance costs.

There are two major languages that are primarily used to develop software systems using object technology: Smalltalk and C++. Of the two, Smalltalk was built from scratch with this paradigm in mind and allows the developer to work at a higher level of abstraction. C++ is a hybrid language where the developer works at a level where she needs to focus on details such as memory management.

Some books have been written that talk about O-O concepts, example uses of the languages, and project war stories, but there is very little guidance on how to rapidly and effectively design and develop production software systems using object technology and/or Smalltalk. That's what this book is about.

Development life-cycle focus for this book

When we talk about developing software more rapidly, there are some constraints that exist. For example, how do we shrink the "setup" and "packaging" portions of the lifecycle? (See figure below.)

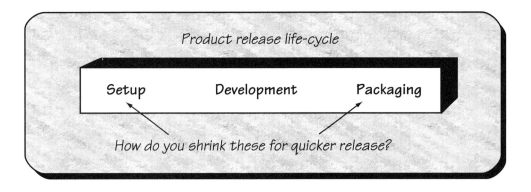

There are certainly changes in your business processes that may reduce the amount of time and effort needed in the setup and packaging portions of the lifecycle. Setup is where you set the general direction for the company, do competitive studies, and plan the funding, staffing, and other issues before a project actually begins. Packaging is where you take the product assets that are ready for a release for commercial sale and take them through product delivery, including producing CD-ROM disks and publishing final page changes for manuals. These phases are outside the scope of this book and will not be addressed here. What we will focus on is the software development portion of the lifecycle, providing guidance on how to reduce the time and effort on the most intensive and expensive portion of the lifecycle.

Case-study application

I have purposely included examples from different business domains, such as retail, telephony, pharmaceuticals, accounting, finance, and manufacturing, in order to make the book more interesting. However, I have also included a case study InventoryManagement application in an appendix and have given many examples drawn from this application throughout the book in order to also have a common thread to follow. For example, the cluster of classes that support mixed currencies can be used in this application.

Contents

Contents

Chapter 1

A rapid development process

I‌T I‌S D‌I‌F‌F‌I‌C‌U‌L‌T to explain what we do in our everyday experiences of delivering successful O-O systems in a short time period. Of necessity, some simplifications are required. Nevertheless, I will attempt to capture in a "cookbook" process the steps to follow. Like using a cookbook, you will be able to follow the recipe to a good meal, but you won't be a chef. With experience will come the confidence and knowledge to improvise, adapt, and create true software culinary experiences.

Processes should be adapted to your situation

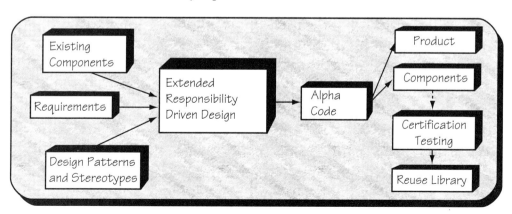

Figure 1.1. Rapid development process overview.

As shown in Figure 1.1, the process starts with a set of requirements, whether in someone's head or on paper. On paper, you can use parts-of-speech techniques* to start extracting candidate classes for your object model. In either case, you will need the domain expert's head in the room during your modeling session as well as someone to decide where the requirement boundaries lie.

As you go about exploring the business domain, you need to remain cognizant about what componentry is available to reuse. These include:

- **Base classes.** All Smalltalk environments include hundreds of classes that are available to reuse. These provide the basic building blocks for the computer domain, such as Integer and Stream.

- **Frameworks.** All Smalltalk environments include multiple frameworks. The most obvious is Model-View-Controller (or some variant). Your company may have patterns that have guided the development of one or more frameworks that you can reuse.

- **Business domain components.** If your company has had previous O-O projects, you should be able to reuse some of the componentry built on those projects. Make sure you don't reinvent the wheel. Pay particular attention to synonyms for the same concepts. This is one of the reasons why a good description for all classes and subsystems is so important.

- **Object models.** Again, if your company has had previous O-O projects, you can probably find whole pieces of models to reuse. Recently, I had the fortune to start working with a new project in a totally different business domain from a project I worked with a couple of years ago. But there was a whole subsystem that I knew we could reuse essentially as-is from a modeling and design standpoint.†

---

*There is some benefit in looking at the nouns, verbs, and adjectives used in your requirements documents. These help identify candidate classes and subsystems, methods, and subclasses respectively. There is not a direct correlation to your object model—experience-based judgement must be used to decide what to do with these candidate objects. This technique is meant to be used to complement other techniques, since it does not by itself scale well to large systems.

†We were fortunate in that this reuse was within the same large company. This would have been a rework if it had been another company. Such is the legal state of reuse.

Responsibility Driven Design (RDD) was documented in Wirfs-Brock (1989) and extended in Lorenz (1993). This methodology, as the name implies, focuses on the behavior of the system as the primary driving factor in its development. It might also be thought of as *Requirements* Driven Design, because it keeps the "what" (i.e., requirements) in the focus until later stages in the lifecycle.

During modeling, you want to succinctly describe your subsystems (groupings of classes), contracts (groupings of public responsibilities), and key classes (essential problem domain concepts) to firm up your business object model quickly in the team member's heads. Once your team has a mental grasp of the basic structure of the business model, progress goes much more quickly with higher quality. Make sure that the names and descriptions are clear and are not redundantly used in other parts of the model.

Use anthropomorphic questioning—"does it make sense for this object to do that?"—when placing responsibilities on classes and subsystems. You can use stereotypes (see Wirfs-Brock, 1994) to help check the accuracy of your choices.

Once you've developed your product, you can harvest reusable componentry for submittal to the company's reuse library.

Requirements analysis

It is important to keep control of an iterative process. This control is effective by driving the effort expended and decisions of completion by documented requirements. This still leaves leeway in what is built. All features take time to build, test, document, and support over the life of the product. As such, we don't want to build any more than we are required to meet our goals. It is easy in a rapid development environment to add little extras as we go. Strong control over the requirements can be maintained by regularly:

Rapid development using an iterative process makes a focus on requirements even more important.

- ♦ **Asking customers:**
  Is this necessary to satisfy our documented requirements?
  Does our competition have this feature? If not, does it provide real value to our customers? Have we asked them?

♦ Showing customers:
Demonstrations of the latest product under development, getting feedback such as features ranked by importance.

Use cases

Use cases are an effective technique for organizing and tracking your requirements.

Use cases are documented in Jacobson (1992). They provide a means for organizing, understanding, and tracing your requirements throughout the development process. Your use cases are a "higher-level" statement of what your system is to do than scenario scripts, which are discussed elsewhere in this book (see Fig. 1.2).

Scenario scripts should relate to the use cases, since use cases document the system requirements. The goal with scenarios is to cover all the key functionality of the system, filling in the object model details. The goal of use cases is to cover all the requirements of the system.

Scenario scripts

Scenario scripts map use cases to the object model under development. There can be multiple scripts for one use case. A script will trace the thread of messaging for a single request through the key classes in the object model as shown in Figure 1.3. This is often referred to as part of the *dynamic model* of the business.

Inventory management

The system will handle the case where a product is below a specified minimum stocking level. When the amount on hand falls below this level, the system will automatically reorder an amount to reach the specified maximum stockcing level.
  Further sales of the product that is out of stock will result in an advance order. In this case, the customer will be called when the item is received. The system should notify the salesperson with a printout of all these advance orders that can now be fulfilled

•••

Figure 1.2. Example partial use case.

Out of Stock
-This scenario handles the case when we reach an out of stock situation for a Product
Product requests amount: anAmount of: myself from **Order**
    Order requests amount: anAmount of: aProduct from **OrderLineItem**
Product sends submit to **Order**
    Order sends for: myself to **OrderForm**
        OrderForm requests productName from **Order**
•••

Figure 1.3. Example of partial scenario script.

Scheduling

Use cases and scenario scripts provide a good basis for scheduling. Since they work with the business domain key classes, the scheduling of the use cases will usually be serial. This is due to the fact that these classes will be owned by the same people across the use case development.

Support classes, such as reporting, database broker, view, and other frameworks, can be built in parallel with the use case development. The goal is to develop the support classes before they're needed for the business domain key classes (see Fig 1.4.).

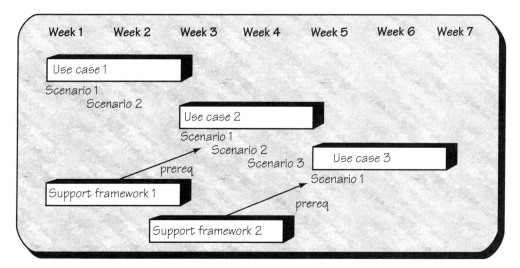

Figure 1.4. Scheduling based on use cases.

Lorenz (1994) details how to estimate the amount of effort for O-O development. He states that for each subsystem:

1. Perform a two-to-ten day domain analysis to find most of the key classes in that area of the system.

2. Categorize your UI from simple (2.0 weighting factor) to complex (3.0 weighting factor).

3. Multiply the number of key classes from (1) above by the weighting factor from (2) above to estimate the total number of classes in the subsystem.

4. Multiply the estimated total number of classes from the previous step by 15 to 20 person-days, depending on factors such as your developers' O-O experience level and number of domain reusable components in the reuse library, to arrive at an early estimate of the total effort necessary to develop the subsystem.

Requirements management

*Managing your requirements is **the** most effective way to deliver your software faster. Iterations facilitate requirements management.*

List the total required functionality at a high level. This may be outputs from business process reengineering (BPR) sessions or an overview section of a requirements document.‡ This will help quickly focus the team's view of what is required and what is not.

Rank the functionality in order of importance. Focusing on higher priority requirements will help you manage the effort. If you need to look at cutting back on requirements to bring in delivery dates, you would start with the requirements with a lower priority ranking.

---

‡Different organizations will need to delve to different levels of detail. For example, a developer on a job for the U.S. government was telling me recently about her customer's desire for great detail in project documentation.

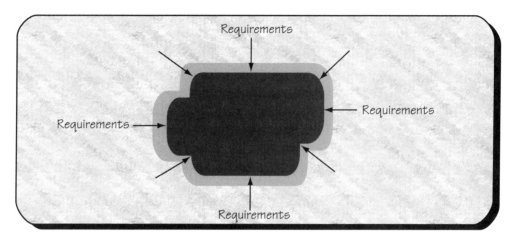

Figure 1.5. Pushing the requirements boundaries inward.

Examine requirement volatility. As Gamma (1994) states, "A thorough requirements analysis will highlight the requirements that are likely to change during the life of the software." If you know which requirements are likely to change in the future, you can plan for flexibility in those areas. This should reduce your future development costs. I also think that it is worth more in-depth questioning in these areas, since some of the expected changes may be due to the fact that users really do not want what is currently viewed as a requirement. Perhaps the expected changes should be made with the *first* release.

Force out any design "requirements" you can. These are usually not really required, but are, instead, someone's view of how they might implement part of the system or how the system has worked traditionally. This is all good documentation, but it should be segregated from the parts that are truly requirements.

Requirements push the system boundaries inward (see Fig. 1.5.). Question exactly what is required of the system and remove anything that is not, such as "feature creep" and "nice to have" comments from the customer.

Estimating accuracy

Keep in mind that as time passes, estimates will get better. You need to iterate on your estimates and project schedule the same as you do for other portions of your project.

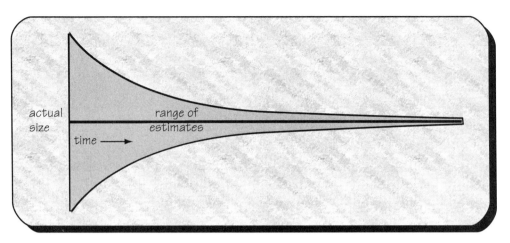

Figure 1.6. Estimating accuracy.

Keeping this accuracy in mind will help you more quickly detect when action plans are needed as your project progresses. (See Fig. 1.6.)

Finding what you need when you need it

You want people on the team to be able to understand the system quickly, locate components to reuse, and locate bugs quickly during development. Many characteristics of methodologies and tools relate to filtering and/or categorizing large volumes of information. We will increase the speed of development by doing the same thing:

♦ **Subsystem.** Collaborating classes of objects that provide related end-user functionality, documented in the form of *contracts*, should be grouped in a subsystem.

♦ **Protocol.** Methods that relate to similar types of services should be grouped in a protocol (also known as a *category*).

♦ **Stereotype.** Wirfs-Brock (1993) discusses the use of stereotypes to categorize roles that objects play. The role may change for a different scenario. Stereotypical behavior, such as active versus passive objects, helps in understanding the system.

♦ **Identifying changes.** A technique in use by multiple groups, including ObjectShare and Hatteras Software, is to add a unique and descriptive symbol (e.g. #modifiedByHatteras) in methods that override base class methods. This symbol can then be searched for via the "senders of" menu item. This is helpful in finding these modifications.

Stereotypes

Wirfs-Brock (1994) talks about her concept of a stereotype. Stereotypes help people to conceptualize and characterize the parts of the object model. As a model develops, the team should start thinking about them in ways that make it easier and easier to decide where responsibilities should reside. Wirfs-Brock (1994) lists the following stereotypes:

♦ **Controlling objects.** These are active objects that drive toward completion of some functionality by collaborating with other objects. An example is a SalesTransaction object in a retail Store.

In our Inventory Management application, the OrderTransaction is the primary active object for Product sales. It moves through the system causing Inventory depletion, participating in invoicing, and so on.

♦ **Coordinating objects.** These objects provide a routing center for messages and services. An example is the Store object, which allows access to Registers and Employees.

For our Inventory Management application, the Company object is the primary coordinator, providing access to customers and Products.

♦ **Structuring objects.** These objects maintain the architected interrelationships between objects.

In our Inventory Management application, the LineItem object maintains the relationship between the OrderTransaction and the Product being sold.

♦ **Informational objects.** These are passive objects that supply values for their client objects. An example is a Customer object that provides its name, address, and phone number.

Similarly, in the Inventory application the Person is a passive supplier of data, such as name and address.

♦ **Service objects.** These are worker bees that do one thing and do it well. An example is a MonthlySalesReport object.

VisaCreditCard and OrderLog are examples of service objects in our Inventory domain.

♦ **Interface objects.** These objects live at the boundaries of the system, talking to end users, equipment, and external systems. Examples are View and BankNetwork objects.

The OrderWindow and Printer are examples of interface objects for the Inventory Management application.

Note that the same object may play different stereotypical roles during different usage scenarios. Using stereotypes is similar in intent to using subsystems and contracts: they provide abstractions that help people deal with the complexities of the system. Stereotypes do not exist in the running system, but are useful characterizations that can be a part of your documentation and certainly should be a part of your mental model of the system.

Types of model objects

It is important to develop a conceptual view of your object model as you develop it. You need to characterize the roles that different objects will play, the relationships they have with other objects, important collaborations, and distribution of responsibilities. Stereotypes help us with the categorization of objects. We can ask ourselves these types of questions when trying to grasp the roles that an object will play in our system:

♦ **Activity**

Is this an active object, causing things to happen?

Is this a passive object, waiting to provide information when asked?

♦ **Longevity**

Does this object live for long periods of time, providing a consistent base of knowledge?

Does this object live for short periods of time? Is its lifetime related to a particular event? Can it be suspended, thereby remaining in the system for longer periods?

♦ **Volume**

How many instances of this object are expected? How many are needed at any one time? Are there any logical groupings?

Design sessions

Rapid modeling and design sessions start out being mostly educational (Fig. 1.7). The technical team has to learn O-O techniques and the O-O consultants have to learn the problem domain. As time goes on, the percentages shift toward more time being spent on actual progress on the object model development.

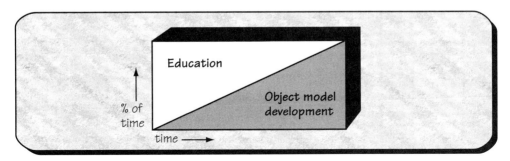

Figure 1.7. Shifting of time usage.

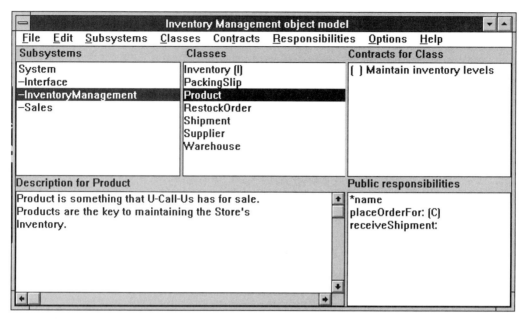

Figure 1.8. Example of object model browser.

The team rapidly moves to prototyping in Smalltalk to verify the model and fill in more details. Often, there are changes to plow back into the modeling sessions.

I prefer to have object model (Fig. 1.8), scenario script (Fig. 1.9), and collaboration diagram (Fig. 1.10) browsers open during the modeling sessions.

The object model browser intentionally leaves off the state data (instance, class, and class instance variables) and private responsibilities.[§] This helps keep us focused on the public behavior during the early modeling sessions, which is the most effective way to develop a good model of your business.

The browser needs to be able to keep up with the fast pace of the modeling sessions. Questions, debates, issues, and decisions are being made at a furious pace. The tools should help, not hinder, this process.

[§]These are included in another browser used later in the modeling.

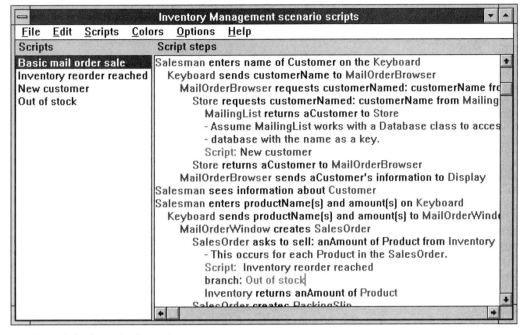

Figure 1.9. Example of script browser.

The script browser allows the message flow for a particular event thread to be documented in time-ordered sequence. Scripts should be able to be reused.

Collaboration diagrams focus on the essential messaging relationships between the subsystems and key classes.

different groups like to work differently, and there is no right way to proceed. My preference is to initially discuss the simplest mainstream scenario possible. As we try to fill in the steps, we flip back to the object model browser, filling in details for the subsystems and classes. We focus on the *behaviors* necessary, trying to fill in contracts first. We ignore state data and private methods as long as possible. As the key classes become clear, due to their central role in the business model, we place them on collaboration diagrams with their contracts indicated.

The design takes shape with a small group rapidly interacting. The important mix of expertise are the business domain and object technology.

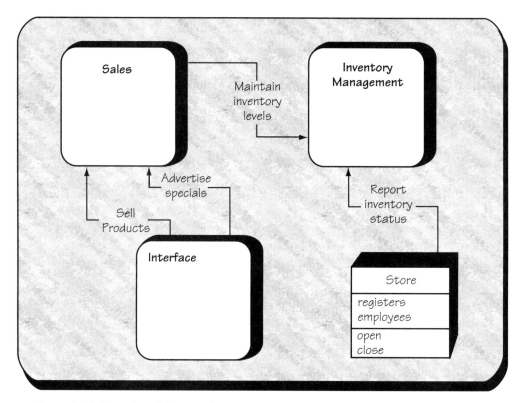

Figure 1.10. Example collaboration diagram.

Bring these two forces together, mix it up with interactive questioning and probing (filling in the details in a tool), and you end up with a solid foundation for your object model.

Design reviews

In order to speed up the development process, focus your design reviews on areas of the system that have anomalies based on O-O metrics (see Fig. 1.11). In this way, you can spend your time on a smaller percentage of the system for your reviews while potentially getting more benefit from the reviews, thereby reaching the same or higher levels of quality.

We have found that metrics analyses are quite good at cutting the volume of information down to a more reasonable level. For example, it is

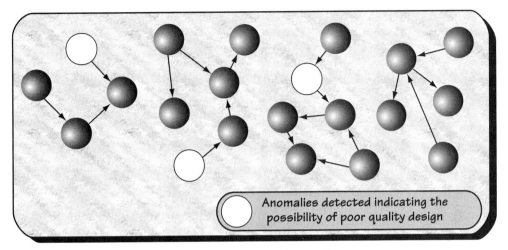

Figure 1.11. Focusing design reviews using metric analysis results.

quite common to have a project with 200 classes and 3,000 methods. To review all of these would take a large amount of time. It is often the case that far less than 10% of the classes result in most of the quality problems (although you will sometimes find poor design techniques running throughout a system). If you can focus your reviews, you can spend half as much time in design reviews and potentially still have five times as much time left for the parts you do review.

Lorenz (1994) recommends the following metrics:

- ◆ **Model quality**

  - ↪ *Hierarchy nesting level.* This is the number of subclassing relationships down from the root class or any framework classes. Numbers over 7 are considered anomalies.

  - ↪ *Global usage.* This is the number of references to unique system-wide globals in a method. It is suggested that no globals be used, but one "system" object as a global is acceptable. Others should be treated as anomalies.

  - ↪ *Commentary.* This is the percentage of commented methods in a class, not counting accessing methods or date-time stamps. Anything below 100% is an anomaly.

♦ Class quality

  ↪ *Number of instance methods.* This is the number of instance methods defined in a class. Numbers over 20 for model classes and 40 for view classes are considered anomalies.

  ↪ *Number of class methods.* This is the number of class methods defined in a class. Numbers over 3 are considered anomalies.

  ↪ *Number of overridden methods.* This is the number of true method overrides in a class, not including framework template methods or method extensions. Numbers over 2 are anomalies.

♦ Method quality

  ↪ *Number of message sends.* This is the number of unary, binary, and keyword messages sent from a method. Numbers over 24 are considered anomalies.

  ↪ *Method complexity.* This is the number of execution path choices plus one, as defined by McCabe, for a method. Numbers over 6 are anomalies.

♦ Management

  ↪ *Number of public instance methods.* This is the total number of instance methods available to clients of a class, which is used to track progress as they are completed.

  ↪ *Problem reports per class.* This is the number of problems found in a class, used to decide when design and requirements reviews are needed.

  ↪ *Effort per class.* This is the number of person-days spent on a class' development. Numbers of around 15 person-days for a production class are typical. This is used for scheduling and estimating.

  ↪ *Classes per developer.* This is the number of classes owned by a developer. Numbers between 20 and 40 are typical and are used for staffing.

Design review checklist

The following list is offered as a starting point for you to customize for your use in performing design reviews.

- ✓ Collection protection is being used to keep clients from accidentally corrupting your objects' state.

- ✓ Accessing methods are being used to facilitate business rules.

- ✓ *Laissez-faire* initialization is being used for more robust designs and easier subclassing.

- ✓ Coding conventions, such as indentation, are being followed to provide better readability.

- ✓ Cleanup of **self halt**, references to **Transcript**, and deadwood code has occurred.

- ✓ All classes, contracts, subsystems, and nonaccessing methods have short, crisp descriptions.

Preparation

Build the support layer before or during the OOA for the business applications. These layers of objects should insulate the business model objects from dealing with the details of persistence, communications, and other environment-support needs. Many of the support layers can and should be purchased rather than built, with your project providing a thin layer to adapt them to your needs, as shown in Figure 1.12. You do not want to be in the database or communications business if you are trying to develop a retail, insurance, or banking application. Focus on your business domain with your resources. There are whole companies doing nothing but DBMS and communications products. Smalltalk and third-party vendors have components you can reuse, often without runtime fees.

Focus on the business processes identified during Business Process Re-engineering (BPR) for your subsystems and required behaviors. If you have

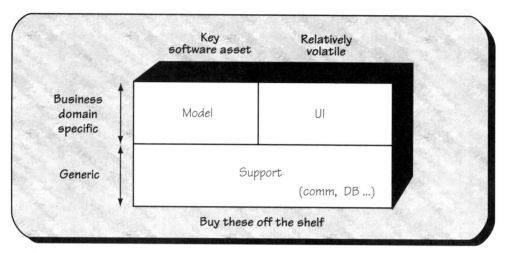

Figure 1.12. Business vs. support layers.

performed a BPR on your business, you have a good start at your requirements and are ready to begin your object modeling effort.

Use mini-prototypes

My friend Steve Lam, whom I believe is an excellent project manager, used an analogy that I liked very much. He said that he uses mini-prototype iterations to "clear the mine fields" so that the project "army" can move through an area unencumbered. So I pass along that advice, which I have seen used successfully on Steve's project.

Target the mini-prototypes in areas you do not understand well or in which you know you have key issues to resolve. These are often in areas such as:

♦ **Concurrency issues for a database.** Can you use optimistic record locking, locking records only when an update is requested, or must you use pessimistic?

Do you have multiple processes working together in a distributed object architecture? This will require coordination and control of object behaviors, since it goes beyond the realm of a single Smalltalk process.

- ◆ **Reuse of componentry across projects.** Do you need to prove the feasibility of reuse of candidate components across multiple projects at your company?

- ◆ **Performance concerns.** Do you have a large number of records in the database that require smart caching or choices of when to instantiate business objects and when to work with simple objects such as Integers and Strings?

- ◆ **Establishing standards.** Do you need to set coding, methodology, process, and other standards for your team?

- ◆ **Clarifying requirements.** Do you have clear requirements?

Iterative process

An important part of speeding up the effective delivery of software systems is an *iterative development process* (IDP). Lorenz (1993) discusses the IDP in detail, but I'll provide a quick review here.

An IDP consists of multiple *iterations,* each of which is composed of planning, production, and assessment phases, as shown in Figure 1.13. An overall project plan for the iterations is created at the beginning of the project. During the planning phase of each iteration, detailed schedules are created for the line items that will be worked on during that iteration. An example schedule is shown in Figure 1.14.

A *line item* is a task assigned to one person to work on during part of the Production phase of an iterative cycle. For example, someone might work on a task named *Customer record lookup,* which is scheduled to take five person-days to implement and unit test.

After the line items are completed during the production phase, the results are examined in the assessment phase. The emphasis of the assessment changes over time. For example, performance is much more important

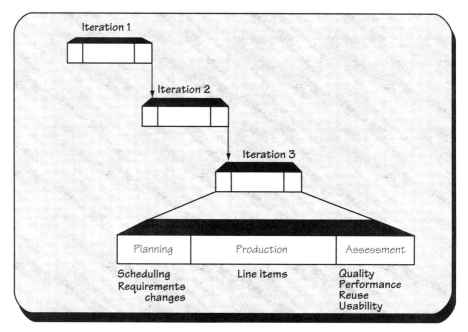

Figure 1.13. Phases of an Iterative Development Process (IDP).

during design than it is during analysis. The results of one iteration's assessment are fed into the planning phase of the next iteration.

	Task Name	13, '94	Nov 20, '94	Nov 27, '94	Dec 4, '94	Dec 11, '
1	**Use case 1**					
2	**Subsystem 1**					
3	Scenario 1			Mark Lorenz,Chris Beasley		
4	Scenario 2				Mark Lorenz,Chris Beasley	
5	**Subsystem 2**					
6	Scenario 1			Bob Brodd,Mark Wynkoop		
7	Scenario 4				Bob Brodd,Mark Wynkoop	
8	**Use case 2**					
9	Scenario 3 Prototype			Wayne Staats		
10	Scenario 3 Unit test				Wayne Staats	
11	Scenario 3 Design review					
12	**Support subsystem 1**					
13	Communications contracts		Tre Poinboeuf			
14	**Support subsystem 2**					
15	Database broker contracts			Denise Lorenz		

Figure 1.14. Sample schedule based on use cases and scripts.

Designs need to be reworked multiple times to achieve high quality. One example is Love (1994), which states that three iterations are optimal. My experience has been that two to six iterations are ideal, with the average being somewhere between three and four. As humorous as it sounds, I've run into many projects that "only have time for one iteration." That is not an iterative process! It is also not an iteration to incrementally add function, although increments are certainly a part of an iteration. True iterations revisit and rework parts of the analysis, design, or both and add new incremental functionality.

Good designs need to be reworked multiple times to become high quality.

Iterations facilitate effective end user feedback, ensuring accurate requirement understand and delivery. It is during the assessment period of the iterations that the users should be involved.

Cycle between modeling and prototyping

Generally, most subsystems need between two days and two weeks to get far enough along on the object model to be ready to start prototyping. You do not need to spend months or years modeling before moving on to prototyping—in fact, you are much better off if you don't! I helped model

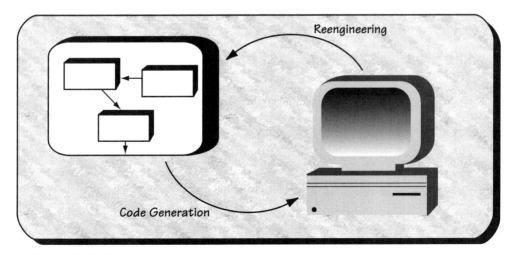

Figure 1.15. Rapid cycling between modeling and ptototyping.

IBM's StorePlace™ product, which was and is a large C++ project. We spent two weeks of solid modeling on the ElectronicTendering subsystem, followed by one week on the Accounting subsystem, and so on. After each modeling segment, the subsystem team moved on to prototyping. That doesn't mean that they didn't revisit the model—they did. But they revisited it with more detailed knowledge grounded in real efforts instead of drawings on a white board. And so the cycle goes until the subsystem's model is solid at which point the cycles stay at the design level.

After your initial rapid modeling sessions, the most effective process is to cycle between prototyping in Smalltalk and additional modeling (see Fig. 1.15). The prototyping helps us discover any important missing details before we go too far and allows better feedback from customers. You should cycle updates back to the essential parts of your object model, as shown in Figure 1.16.

It is not recommended that all details in your development environment be put in your model. Private methods, peripheral helper classes, numerous framework subclasses should not be included. These detailed design aspects only get in the way when you are trying to understand the key parts of your business.

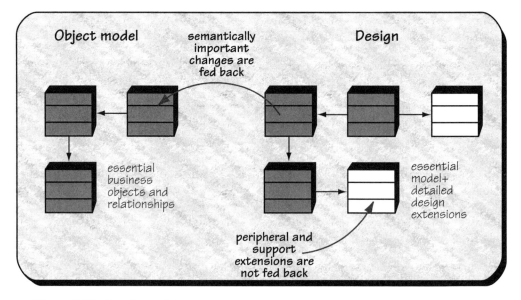

Figure 1.16. Modeling and design synchronization.

You want to use tools that will generate code based on your object model, and allow you to capture changes in the development image to update with the model.

This cycle keeps the two effs in sync with each other, allowing quick movement between different levels of detail—from the abstract modeling to the concrete prototyping.

Modeling

During your modeling sessions, model broadly and develop subsystems relatively independently (Fig. 1.17). A broad perspective makes sure you accurately reflect your business so you don't get into trouble later by having a narrow focus.

Model more broadly than your development focus to ensure a solid foundation for future releases.

Even though you model broadly, you don't have to develop all the subsystems at once. Once you accurately capture your business in an object model, you can decide to implement some portions of the model, delaying other portions until later releases.

Projects will often work across multiple subsystems with a core group of architects and different groups from the subsystem teams (Fig. 1.18). The architecture group brings a broad view to the modeling sessions. The subsystem teams have a more parochial view and focus on their internal structure and how they will service their subsystem-level contracts.

Focus on the model objects and ignore the interface objects as long as possible. People always seem to want to think in terms of the user interface

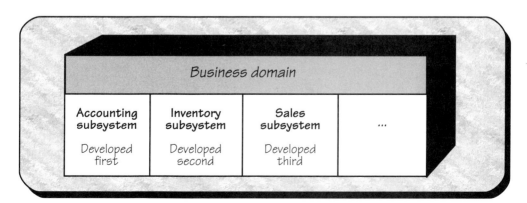

Figure 1.17. A modeling strategy.

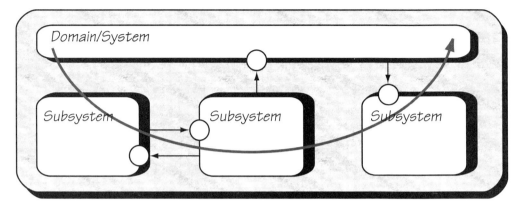

Figure 1.18. Round-robin analysis across an architecture.

and/or the current database design. Resist these impulses until you have a solid object model that meets your needs. You will end up with a model that is more extensible and reusable this way.

For example, if you include your InventoryManagement subsystem in your modeling, even though you are not going to automate it until the next release, you can develop a model that will handle the future addition of this subsystem more easily (see Fig. 1.19).

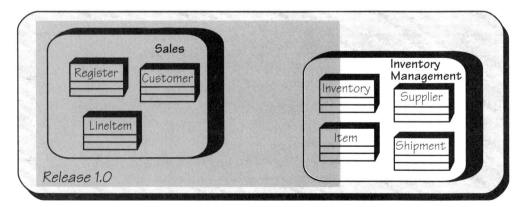

Figure 1.19. Planning for future releases.

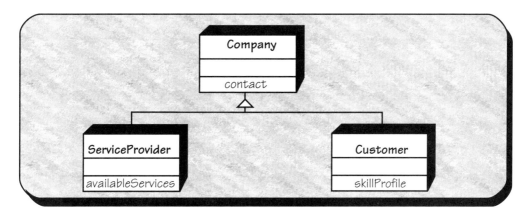

Figure 1.20. Example of single-minded classes.

By including Inventory and Item objects in your model, you are laying the groundwork for a future release to include a subsystem that will maintain its own inventory levels. Adding this subsystem will be relatively painless, since your original modeling and prototyping planned for this major part of your business domain. The point is that release contents should not drive your modeling, the business domain should.

A modeling dilemma

When developing an object model, there is a trade-off to be made between two conflicting goals:

- **Single-minded objects.** My rule of thumb is to err on the side of defining larger numbers of smaller classes. This strategy tends toward objects that are very straightforward in what they do and how they behave. They are what I call "single-minded."

  For example, in a vendor management application I may have ServiceProvider and Customer objects as specializations of Company, as shown in Figure 1.20. They include only those portions of what it is to be their type of Company and are therefore simpler.

- **Flexibility of roles.** Classes of objects that have the ability to play different roles are more flexible in how they can be used. They can be placed in different situations simultaneously or subsequently. The developer does not have to worry about data updates across different instances that relate to each other, instantiating another variant of an object because of the usage, or "morphing" an object into another type of object due to the situation.

For example, in the vendor management system I could have a **Company** class of objects that knows how to be a service provider as well as a customer (see Fig. 1.21). The same **Company** could in fact be both at the same time. This class is more difficult to build, but depending on the system requirements the overall system may be simpler due to this flexibility.

Figure 1.21. Example of more flexibility in roles.

Of course, as is explored elsewhere in this book, you can alternatively create **Role** objects to collaborate with the domain objects to explicitly deal with these roles. This choice should be based on what behaviors the **Roles** would play. For example, **Roles** often help with system authorizations and access. If you don't have any real behavior for the **Roles**, don't create a separate class.

The choice really depends on the domain requirements. If you think there is a good chance that the roles that the objects will play will not vary for any one type of object, then you should choose the simpler single-minded modeling. If you think that the roles could vary, then you should choose the more flexible modeling.

For example, if one **Company** can provide services as well as request services, then you will want the **Company** class to be able to play both roles. If one **Company** can never be both a **ServiceProvider** and a **Customer**, then you will want to create these specialized subclasses of **Company**.

Script writing

Start with the most mainstream script you can identify. For a mail-order inventory system, it might be *Basic mail order sale*. For a telephony system, it might be *Local phone call*. Stick initially to the most straightforward path, merely identifying alternative paths without following them yet (Fig 1.22).

Script writing is an effective technique for developing your business object model.

Expect the first script to take the longest. You have the least model in the tools or in your head to reuse to help you move faster. Once you complete the first basic mainstream script, you will have gone a long way toward defining the key classes in your system!

Script-writing takes your requirements and use cases and examines how they map to your object model under development. As you write scripts, you will fill in details of the model and validate with your domain experts that your model will meet the requirements.

Why is scripting faster?

Rasmus (1994) discusses the ways that people retain domain knowledge and how we can extract that knowledge. He categorizes knowledge into the following types:

♦ **Declarative.** Superficial facts, such as color and texture

♦ **Procedural.** Step-by-step procedures of how to do something

♦ **Semantic.** Underlying concepts and relationships

♦ **Episodic.** Sequences that are replayed to perform a task

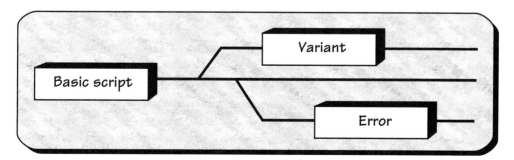

Figure 1.22. Scripting strategy.

Scenarios are effective ways to relate all but declarative knowledge, which is the least useful anyway since they deal only with superficial facts. The point is that scenarios are effective at documenting expertise while working with domain experts. They are an organized way to ask the on-going stream of questions about the domain, filling in details in the object model along the way.

An example basic script

Let's take an example from an inventory management system. The simplest mainstream script¶ we can imagine might be one for a basic mail-order sale, where everything is in stock and the customer has bought from us before.

Notice that in the script in Figure 1.23, we have identified:

- ♦ **Many candidate classes.** Since this is a mainstream scenario, a number of these classes will be key classes that play an important role in the business model.

- ♦ **Subsystems.**

- ♦ **Behaviors.** The behavior of the system is the important aspect to focus on at this point. It is fine to collect other information, such as state data, but stay focused primarily on behavior. Contracts between subsystems and key classes are an abstraction that will help you conceptualize the system.

- ♦ **Variant scripts.** As you go, note other scenarios, leaving them for later exploration. Stick to the simplest flow—it will be involved enough to keep you busy!

- ♦ **Error scripts.** Not all errors are worth documenting in a script. Those that are can be included as you go.

Once you have your basic script, you can work on variants on the theme. Go back to the paths you skipped while completing the initial script. In the example, you might want to explore the *New customer* scenario next.

¶The example uses a format from the HOMSuite modeling tool.

Basic mail order sale
-This scenario is the main usage of the system.
Salesman answers phone
Salesman enters name of Customer on the Keyboard
  Keyboard sends customerName to MailOrderBrowser
    MailOrderBrowser requests customerNamed: customerName from Store
      Store requests customerNamed: customerName from MailingList
        MailingList returns a Customer to Store
        -Assume MailingList works with a Database class to access a customer
        -database with the name as a key.
        Script: Now customer
      Store returns aCustomer to MailOrderBrowser
    MailOrderBrowser sends aCustomer's information to Display
Salesman sees information about Customer
Salesman enter productName(s) and amount(s) on Keyboard
  Keyboard sends productName(s)and amount(s) to MailOrderWindow
    MailOrderWindow creates SalesOrder
      Sales Order asks to sell: an Amount of Product from inventory
      -This occurs for each Product in the SalesOrder
      Script: Inventory reorder reached
      Branch: Out of stock
      Inventory returns anAmount of Product
    SalesOrder creates PackingSlip
    PackingSlip prints Product location(s), Customer name, address on Printer
    SalesOrder prints Product name(s), Customer name, address on Printer
    -Warehouse personnel use PackingSlip to get the Products.
    -Warehouse personnel attach SalesOrder hardcopy to the box.

Legend:
- Dash("-") signifies a comment
- Embedded scripts are indicated by "Script:<name>". These are like macro expansions
- Branches to other scripts are indicated by "Branch:<name>". Those are like "go to"s.

Figure 1.23. Example of scenario script.

During the script-writing, have your model browser open. When you come to a point where you identify a new class, subsystem, or behavior enter the information into your model browser. You should find yourself moving rapidly between your script and model browsers as you discuss the system in modeling sessions.

We like to have an LCD panel with the screen projected onto the wall. A second projector with a transparency and marking pens (or a drawing tool like Visio projected on the wall) also comes in handy to draw collaboration diagrams as you go.

Build in flexibility

Suggest future possibilities to make sure the system handles them well. The required changes may or may not be included in the first delivery, but will certainly happen during the lifetime. This will take more time initially, but will often save time a month or two later when unexpected changes are needed.

Ask questions like:

> Would you ever want to _____?

> What happens if we were to reuse this to _____?

Plan for the possibilities in the initial design. It will force you to build in more reuse and flexibility.

Stop when you understand how to continue

Create scenario scripts and fill in object model details until you understand the business domain well enough to continue to the downstream activities, such as implementation. Extra scripts and object model details are great, but they are not required to get on with the business of a product release.

Make sure you describe the essential characteristics of your objects before continuing. It is important that the conceptual view of the objects is clear in the developers' minds or they won't be able to use effective techniques such as anthropomorphism.[**]

[**] *Anthropomorphism* means "to attribute human qualities to something." A useful technique is to role-play the parts of key objects and see how they would behave in the system under development. You should hear comments such as "it doesn't make sense for a **Product** to do that!" This is a useful way to perform a sanity check on the distribution of responsibilities.

Document as you go

Much of the system can be captured in a textual form. Our experience has been that 10 –15% of the system documentation should be graphical. This provides a high-level view of the system and also helps team members who are more picture oriented.

On projects without expensive CASE tools, we use Visio™ along with our RDD "smart shapes" to draw collaboration and container relationship diagrams for the subsystems and their key classes.

Reengineer to resync

Tools should be used to resynchronize the differences between the model and the implementation under development. HOMSuite™ is our product that facilitates resynchronization between a development image and an object model. It does this by presenting the differences to the user and allowing the user to choose changes to make to the model and development image. This is critical to facilitate rapid traversal between development foci (see Fig. 1.24). You need to try things out and discover more details and issues as early as possible.

Create an analysis prototype first

Even though you will discuss design issues early in the process, don't get tied up with detailed design issues such as storing and retrieving objects in

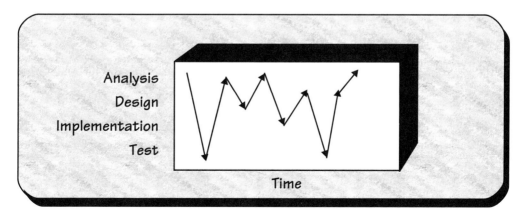

Figure 1.24. Rapid traversal between development foci.

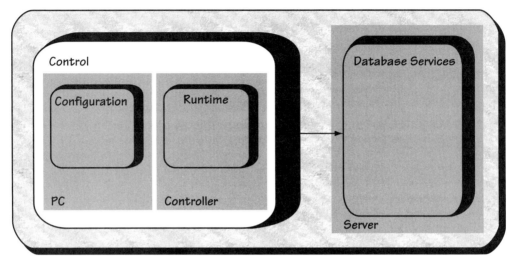

Figure 1.25. Physical mapping of your logical model.

a relational database. Assume infinite time and resources. As long as the system responds in a reasonable fashion during development, we shouldn't focus on performance yet. Our guess at where the performance problems will be will probably be wrong until we can establish an analysis object model. This requires at least a few weeks of modeling effort before we worry

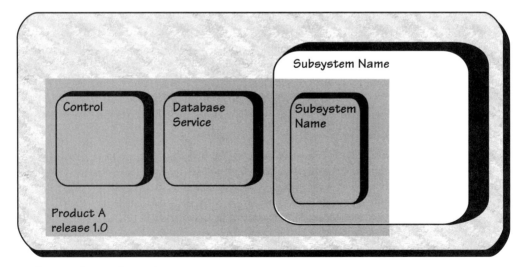

Figure 1.26. Product packaging.

about performance issues. And even then, only the risk areas should be dealt with. Regular performance tuning should wait until the assessment periods of the iterations.

Mapping a Physical Model to your Logical Model

The physical grouping of the logical components of your object model into runtime files such as executables and dynamic link libraries usually includes whole subsystems at one of the levels, as shown in Figure 1.25.

You can annotate your diagrams with an indication of which processor a particular subsystem or group of subsystems will reside. You can carry this further to indicate individual EXE or DLL files in larger, more complex systems.

Product Packaging

As with the physical mapping, indicating groupings of componentry to include in a product release is helpful (see Fig. 1.26). Normally, this will include versions of components that make up the configuration.

Chapter 2

Methodology overview

I AM A STRONG supporter of behavior-driven methodologies. The reasons for this support are numerous—I'll list a few:

Focus on the behavior of your system before you worry about attributes or persistence.

- ◆ *"Overly centralized control leads to a procedural style of problem decomposition." (Wirfs–Brock, Nov. 1993)*

    An intelligent object model needs to be able to take care of its own business. Activities cannot be driven by a central "manager" object, UI sequence, or work flow and have intelligent objects in the model deciding what they need to do to enforce the business rules for your company. What is a model object to do when it decides that some action is needed, but the "sequence from hell" is waiting to carry out its next step?!

- ◆ We need to focus on the distribution of behavior across the object model in order to manage the complexities of the system. A data focus does not do this.

    Think about how you deal with your everyday world: you wake up to an alarm clock, turn it off, get up and let the dog out, get your daughter started dressing, get your e-mail on your computer, start the coffee pot, remind your wife about a PTA meeting you both are going to that night.... In other words, you interact with all kinds of objects, many of which handle numerous details for you while you go on about your business. You don't make steering corrections for the people on the interstate highway while you fix coffee! You don't tell your dog how to walk, your daughter how to dress, and your wife how to talk (well, maybe)!

♦ Data-driven approaches result in more complex systems.
Wirfs-Brock, Nov.–Dec., 1994 examines the same application developed by Boeing using a Shlaer/Mellor approach, which is more data-driven, to an RDD approach using the MIT O-O software metrics. The measurements indicated that the RDD system had less messaging to achieve the same functionality.

♦ People can understand a behavior approach. Simple techniques such as script writing relate closely to object behaviors. Architected contract interfaces between subsystems have been effectively used many times on large commercial projects to divide up the work while keeping control of the development.

No matter what methodology you choose, I strongly suggest you focus on the required behaviors of the system. The main documented behavior-driven methodologies today are Wirfs-Brock (1990), Jacobson (1992), and Lorenz (1993). My overriding question for deciding whether something deserves its own class or not is this: What *behavior* does this object provide? If the object doesn't really provide any interesting behavior in the problem domain, then it is probably just an instance of some base class held as an attribute in a domain class.

For example, perhaps a Customer has an "address." Well, is "address" a new class, or is it an instance of an existing base class, such as String?

♦ What if all we do with "addresses" is print them out on letters to our Customers? We could use a String to support this requirement. (See the second part of Fig. 2.1.)

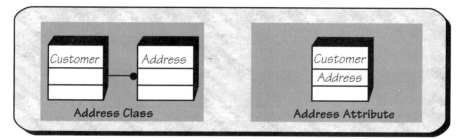

Figure 2.1. Alternative models for "address."

♦ What if we use an "address" to help decide the best shipping routes for our trucks? With this added behavior, we will want an **Address** class. (See the first part of Fig. 2.1.)

Many O-O methodologies, including Coad and Rumbaugh, place a high level of interest on the data, which is a strong temptation for novice O-O developers anyway. Former E/R modelers are especially tempted to keep modeling the database. This is certainly a key part of any project and very important—it is just not the most important activity and will get in the way greatly during the system object model analysis.

The most effective methodology is actually a mixture of methodologies. Our mix looks something like Figure 2.2:

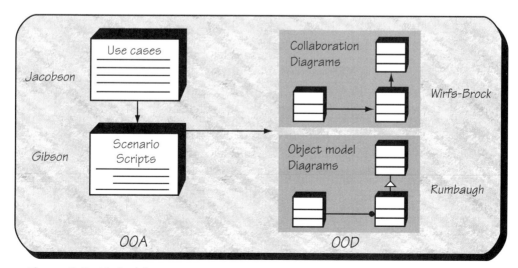

Figure 2.2. Methodology mix.

We take the best portions of the best methodologies and use them in combination:

♦ Jacobson's use cases for requirements analysis

♦ Gibson's scenario scripts for object model discovery based on required behaviors

♦ Wirfs-Brock's collaboration diagrams for architecting the system and maintaining a behavior focus

♦ Rumbaugh's object diagrams for container and specialization relationships

Table 2.1 lists the activities and deliverables of the different phases of the methodology.

Table 2.1. Methodology activities and deliverables.

Prerequisites	Activities	Deliverables
Analysis		
Requirements	*Document requirements* 　Write use cases	Use case document
Use case document	*Discover an initial object model* 　Write scenario scripts 　Draw collaboration diagrams 　　(messaging relationships) 　Define classes, subsystems, 　　and contracts 　Draw object model diagrams 　　(container relationships)	Skeleton code Updated use cases Collaboration diagrams Design documentation Scenario scripts Object model diagrams
Code from object model	*Validate the object model* 　Analysis prototyping	Updated object model Usability feedback
Design		
Validated object model	*Develop the system* 　Design subsystems 　Develop classes 　Run function tests	Production subsystems
Production subsystems	*Integrate the system* 　Run integration tests	Integrated subsystems

While developing your system using this methodology, think of your objects as self-managing, living things in your system. This anthropomorphic view will help you more effectively assign responsibilities to the classes of objects. For example, you might ask yourself or your team members questions like

♦ Does it make sense for **anAccount** to **deposit:** anAmount and withdraw: anAmount? Yes.

♦ Does it make sense for **anAccount** to **printStatement**? No, but it should provide information to **aReport** object to produce the statement.

What this does for you is cause you to build an object model that has more reuse potential. In fact, one good way to verify your choices is to see how other clients of a class of objects would reuse the services. If there is a need to rewrite some of the code in other clients' methods, then perhaps that logic should be moved to the server class' method. If there is a need to work through other objects to indirectly get to the desired service, then perhaps one or more methods are in the wrong place and should be reassigned.

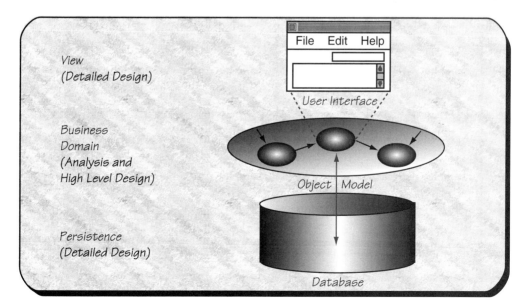

Figure 2.3. Separation of the model from views and persistence.

Once you get a foundation for your business object model, you will be ready to focus on a user interface that will allow the user to control the model in an effective manner (Fig. 2.3).

Finally, but certainly not unimportantly, focus on the storage details of the model objects. In some systems, the data that will make up objects will come from other non–O-O systems already in production. This will present a nontrivial challenge to instantiate enough of your model to support the O-O part of the system. It is possible, but this is a practical fact of life to be aware of as you start migrating pieces of your business software to object technology.

Collaboration diagrams

People cannot deal with the complexities of today's software systems. We need abstractions and containers to help us manage the voluminous details. We use a layered approach to documenting the most important software assets, as in Figure 2.4.

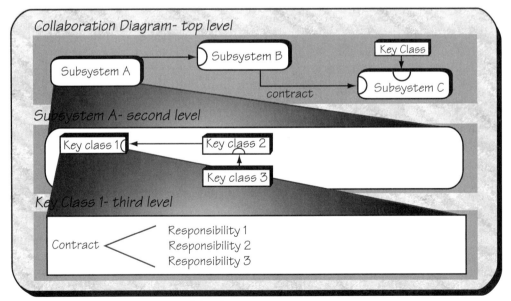

Figure 2.4. Modeling layers of detail.

Layering occurs at each level of detail:

♦ At the top level, classes and lower-level subsystems are primarily grouped into functionally related categories called *subsystems.* Contracts between the subsystems and a few cross-subsystem key classes are shown.

    For example, Inventory and Product classes might be grouped into the InventoryManagement subsystem since they are involved in the identified high-level support contracts Maintain inventory levels and Report inventory status. The contracts were identified by asking questions such as

   ↪ *Why do we need this subsystem?*

   ↪ *What is it required to do?*

   ↪ *What are the primary responsibilities of this part of the system?*

   ↪ *Does that make sense for this subsystem to do that, or should another subsystem do it?*

♦ At the next level, contractual relationships between key business domain classes[*] and possibly lower-level subsystems are shown.

    This level of detail is filled in during rapid modeling sessions, where scenario scripts for the subsystem are written based on the use cases (which are based on the requirements).

♦ At the lower level, detailed public responsibilities for contracts within a class are shown.

    For example, the contract Maintain inventory levels might include receiveShipment:, sell:, and deplete: responsibilities.

This approach allows a developer to view the system at different levels of detail, ignoring portions that are not currently of interest. It also keeps the focus on the distribution of behavior of the system, which is very important.

---

[*] We usually limit our diagrams to key classes, which play an important role in the business domain. There is little gain and definite loss in clarity from including other classes on the diagrams.

Develop your system architecture

Use contracts between subsystems to architect your system.

This may sound obvious, but many projects have no real model and architecture in place or people to manage them.

For our systems, the contracts between subsystems provide the basic system architecture (see Fig. 2.5). These public interfaces are the vehicle by which separate groups can encapsulate each other's work and treat it as a black box.

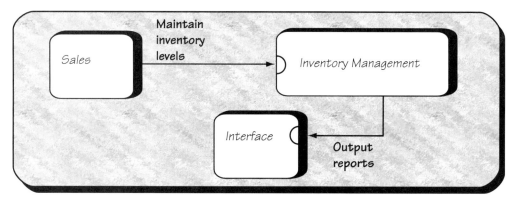

Figure 2.5. Contracts in a collaboration diagram.

The contracts are owned and controlled by the project architects. The architects negotiate changes to these cross-subsystem interfaces. Note that subsystems can contain other subsystems, so you need to take a look at how your organization matches up to the subsystem structure to decide where ownership lies. For example, lower-level subsystem interfaces could be owned by the technical leads in charge of delivering a subsystem that contains the lower-level subsystem(s).

Architecting large O-O projects

Managing the complexity of most commercial O-O projects requires planning for and controlling an architecture for your business object model. This involves dividing up your system into subsystems, assigning contracts between the subsystems, and establishing your architects' ownership of the contracts.

Figure 2.6 shows a partial project architecture along with high-level ownership assignments. Development teams own particular subsystems and are responsible to build these subsystems so that they support the subsystem contracts. These contracts, such as Maintain inventory levels, provide a set of public services to the other subsystems. The client subsystem teams treat the server subsystem as a black box, ignoring the complexities inside.

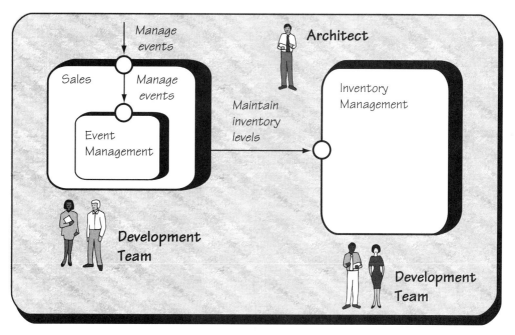

Figure 2.6. Ownership assignments.

This organization allows the development teams to proceed relatively independently of each other, an essential requirement for large projects.

An architecting process

So, how does this architecture come about? Many times, project teams do not have a good idea of what subsystems exist ahead of time. The subsystems, much like other abstractions such as frameworks and abstract classes, become apparent as the system exploratory process proceeds.

Figure 2.7 gives an overview of the process for one subsystem:

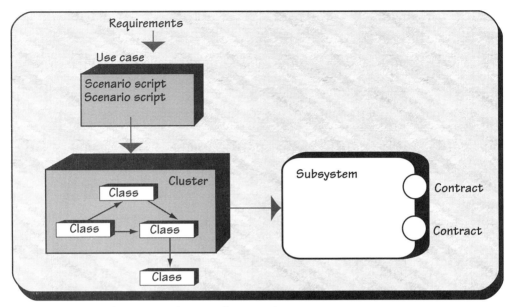

Figure 2.7. Exploring an architecture for one subsystem.

- Use cases are written for the system requirements.

- Scenario scripts are used as a technique to fill in details of the object model.

- Key classes are clustered into more closely coupled groups, called *subsystems*.

- Subsystems are assigned public contracts from groupings of key responsibilities of the classes.

- Development teams are assigned ownership of the subsystems. Their focus is on building a subsystem that supports its contracts.

- Architects are assigned ownership of the subsystem contracts. Their focus is on controlling any changes to the subsystem contracts.

Figure 2.8 shows how the architecture team moves across all subsystems of the system problem domain, working with each of the subsystem teams to model their portion of the system at a high level.

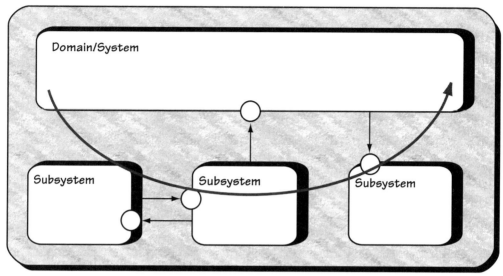

Figure 2.8. Traversing the system.

The contracts between each of the subsystems that make up the system are discovered during rapid modeling sessions of two to ten days each, depending on the subsystem size. Questions such as the following help to identify the subsystem contracts:

- ♦ Why do we have this subsystem?

- ♦ What basic services should it provide?

- ♦ Does it make sense for this subsystem to provide this service?

- ♦ What services does this subsystem need from other subsystems?

Once the rapid modeling session has been completed for one subsystem, its team is free to start iterative development in parallel with other efforts. The development team must negotiate subsystem-level contract changes with the architects, who have a broad, system-wide perspective. The architects will involve affected subsystem owners in the change negotiations.

A Managed Process

Figure 2.9 shows the interrelationships of the deliverables of the architecture development process, which repeats within each of the subsystems.

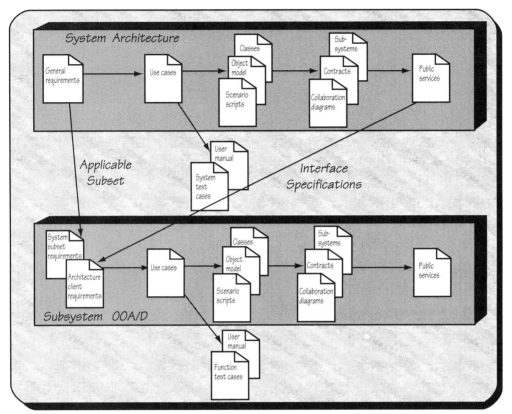

Figure 2.9. An O-O architected development process.

The System Architecture

In developing an architecture, there are a number of steps to follow to consistently and effectively produce a system of a significant size. Although these steps are discussed here in a specific order, be aware that many can be run concurrently, cyclically, or in a somewhat reverse order than presented here. The tasks are presented in a common logical order, but you will find yourself adapting the process to your needs, as well you should.

As we've discussed, you write use cases from the requirements. At a system level, these use cases will provide the inputs for system test cases as well as a user manual. They lead to the production of related dynamic scenario scripts as we've seen before. These scripts help us discover the static relationships between classes in an object model for your business.

As you build up some volume of system objects, you will begin grouping classes into subsystems and, most importantly for large systems, defining public messaging interfaces, called contracts, between the subsystems.

Subsystem Analysis and Design

The system-level contracts define the required interface specifications for each of the top-level subsystems. These contractual requirements, along with an applicable subset of the overall requirements, define the subsystem requirements. The process followed at the system level is followed at the subsystem level for its development.

Since subsystems can contain other subsystems, this "leveling" continues through as many levels as necessary to adequately define the system. Naturally, more complex systems have more levels.

Ownership

The integrity and delivery of the pieces of architecture require that ownership be established. This ownership differs depending on the role (Fig. 2.10).

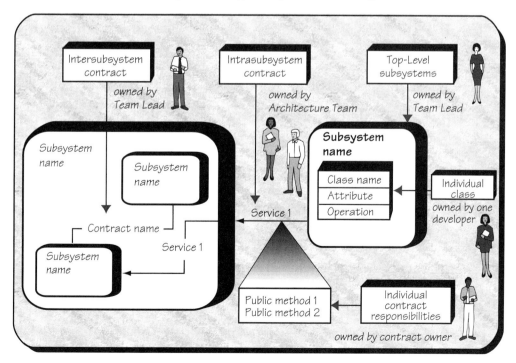

Figure 2.10. Architecture ownership.

◆ **Architect.** An architect owns the *intersubsystem* contracts. This primarily means that the architect controls the definition of the contractual messages required between the top-level subsystems. The architect negotiates with the subsystem owners whenever changes to the interface are requested.

   Architects on large projects are often actually part of a team of architects. Architects often (and quite efficiently) take on the role of the team lead of one of the top-level subsystems.

◆ **Team lead.** A team lead owns the *intrasubsystem* contracts. The team lead is responsible for delivering the functionality to satisfy the intersubsystem contracts and controls the interfaces between the subsystem's developers.

◆ **Developer.** Individual developers construct the classes in the subsystem under the direction of the team lead.

Actively manage your model structure

Most of the systems we develop have one "system" object.[†] The system object is the bootstrap point for the product, providing startup initialization and access to collections of more globally known objects. For example, in retail the Store might hold the Registers and the Employees.

   Below the system object, a basic structure between the key objects in the domain evolves. This structure models the salient relationships in your business domain and will greatly affect your software objects' relationships and how they go about their business.

   In general, you want to keep coupling to one level out from any particular object (see Fig. 2.11). For example, if you take the perspective of aKeyObjectType2, it should only talk directly to aKeyObjectType1 and/or aKeyObjectType3 (which may talk to another layer out to service their requests). In this way, the system's objects have direct or indirect access to all

---

[†]This system object may reside as a global or may be passed around as a parameter. The system may be a domain object, such as a Store in the retail domain, or may be the name of your system, such as OOMetric.

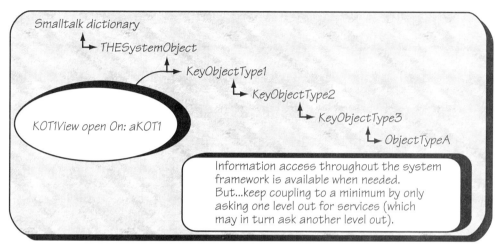

Figure 2.11. Object model relationships.

of the important knowledge in the domain while keeping their coupling at an optimal level. If your distribution of responsibilities is done well, this strategy will provide a good foundation for your model.

View objects can be created at each level of object in the structure (Fig. 2.12). The structure allows the view to present different levels of model information as necessary. Views are generally created via an openOn: message with a parameter containing the key model object they work most closely with (Fig. 2.13).

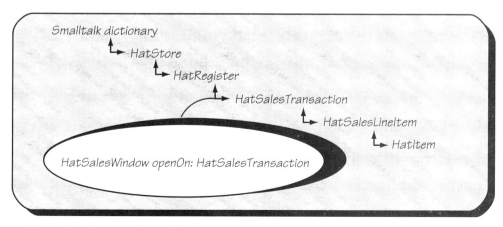

Figure 2.12. Example model structure.

```
InvLobby

sellProducts
  "get the customer information before selling Products"

    InvCustomerWindow new openOn: self company.


InvCustomerWindow

checkCredit
  "make sure the customer has a good credit record before selling Product"

    InvCreditWindow new openOn: self customer.
```

Figure 2.13. Example method coupling according to the Law of Demeter.

Law of Demeter

The law of Demeter defines what is good and bad coupling. The differentiation is based on how easy the code will be to maintain; in other words, how dependent it is on other designs and, thus, how brittle it is. The law states that acceptable coupling consists of messages to:

- ♦ self
- ♦ super
- ♦ Created objects
- ♦ Parameters
- ♦ An object's class

Unacceptable coupling consists of messages to:

- ♦ Globals
- ♦ Return values from messages

The idea is that you don't want to be dependent on other object's designs or have any more knowledge past your "closely related" objects, such as objects they collaborate with that you may indirectly get access to. For example, if you string message sequences together, you could traverse the model relationships and interact with a large number of different types of objects.

Take a look at the Account withdraw: method in Figure 2.14.

```
Account
withdraw: anAmount
    "subtract anAmount from my balance"

| newBalance |
( anAmount > self balance )              "OK - a parameter passed to me"
    ifFalse: [ "error handling for negative values" ].
( super loan payment: anAmount )   "OK - my superclass"
newBalance := self balance - anAmount.
( newBalance := 0.0)                     "OK - I created newBalance"
    ifTrue: [ self owner transactions add: anAmount ]
                "NOT OK! I have assumed an implementation
                 for my owners transaction collection"
    ifFalse: [ self checkOverdraft. ].   "OK - my service"
```

Figure 2.14. Example method coupling according to the Law of Demeter.

In Figure 2.14, the self owner transactions add: anAmount code has assumed an implementation. In this case, it has assumed that the transactions are kept in an OrderedCollection or some other object that understands add:. A more robust design would do something more like:

    self owner addTransactionFor: anAmount

and let the Account's owner take care of its own design details.

Similarly, I could ask the Account's owner for its Bank, then ask the Bank for its employees, and so on. This type of coupling is not good, since the code breaks when an implementation changes. It also makes no sense for the Account object to get into other object's responsibilities. This type of design leads to bugs that result in inappropriate model states.

Architecture document outline

The following outline lists topics you should include in your architecture documentation:

♦ **Process overview.** This section walks the reader through the activities used in developing the O-O system, including techniques and goals.

◆ **Roles.** This section discusses the various roles, such as architect and team lead, that exist on the project. Ownership and authority are discussed as they relate to the system architecture components.

◆ **Architectural overview.** This section discusses the architectural components, how to use the individual subsystem sections that follow, and shows the system-level collaboration diagram.

◆ **Top-level subsystems.** Each of these sections covers one subsystem at a top-level contractual basis.

↪ *Collaboration diagram.* This diagram shows all the required public services provided by the subsystem. Services required from other subsystems are also shown.

↪ *Contracts.* This section describes each contract the subsystem provides and lists expected clients. Individual methods that are a part of the contract are listed and described.

◆ **Subsystem 1 to N.** These sections, which may be packaged as separate documents, detail the internal architecture of each subsystem in the same way as the overall system architecture.

Team composition

Get the right people for your team. Who is right for this effort? There's no correct answer, but there are characteristics to look for:

- **Receptive to change.** There is no better description of moving to O-O than change. It is a very different way of thinking about building software. Those who have built a power structure about themselves based on the current way of doing things are going to resist a field-leveling technology like O-O. Look for people who are confident in themselves and secure in their position in the organization.

- **Fast learner.** This is a good asset in anyone. It is especially good where there is so much to learn. O-O requires a much greater learning curve then moving to another 3GL, for example. In fact, I often think of O-O as an *unlearning* process. Experienced developers have learned to be successful in the function-oriented way of developing software. They must unlearn what they've been doing for years in order to rebuild a new basis for thinking about developing software.

♦ **Think abstractly as well as concretely.** This is essential in a good
O-O developer. I can't think of a single person I consider a solid
O-O developer who doesn't have this skill. Not everyone does.
Thinking abstractly will help enormously in creating frameworks
and using them effectively. Using inheritance effectively almost
requires this capability.

There are differences between:

♦ Who the system is for

♦ Who is buying the system

♦ Who is acceptance testing the system

♦ Who is giving opinions about the system

♦ Who knows the strategic business directions

Make sure you stick to the requirements when you are listening to discussions. Make sure you know who the decision makers are.

Lorenz (1993) stated that you can characterize what your potential team members will be most comfortable doing on your project by getting them evaluated using a method developed by Kathy Kolbe (see Kolbe, 1990). This allows you to ensure that you have a good mix of people. Often, organizations tend toward similar types of people, which results in less optimal use of personnel.

Once you get your team, keep them. There is nothing more disruptive than to have people on your project pulled out to seed other projects. Make sure this transition takes place after you ship. I have seen projects lose calendar months due to the loss of key people who are replaced by novices who not only don't contribute right away, but take time from the experienced members to mentor them.

One thing I have noticed is that certain people work well with certain other people. When you find these combinations, maintain them from project to project.

Team roles

There are a number of roles on an O-O project. Figure 3.1 shows an organization that has been used effectively on multiple commercial O-O projects.

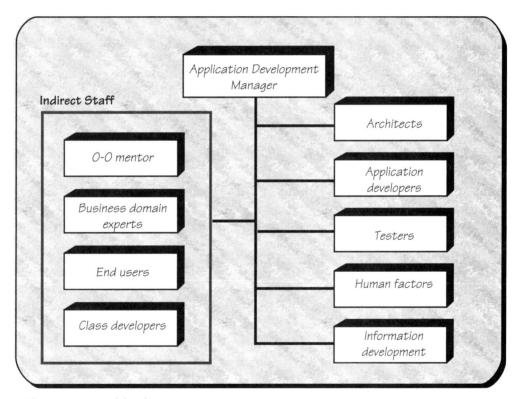

Figure 3.1. High-level project organization.

This is a high-level view of the roles on the project team. If we step another level down in detail (see Fig. 3.2), focusing on the architecture of the application being developed, we can organize our people along compatible lines with the software being developed.

The project needs one or more people to keep a cross-system view and control of the interfaces between the different subsystem teams. These are the architects.

Organize your team along the same lines as your software architecture.   Each subsystem needs a technical lead to be responsible for building the subsystem to support its contractual interfaces. This lead will normally have one or more people working for her. They will own the classes in the subsystem.

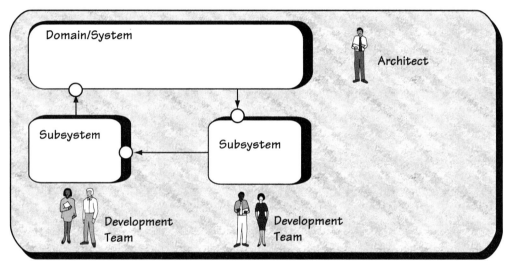

Figure 3.2. Detailed project organization.

I'll discuss some of the most important roles in this section. Keep in mind that a role does not equal a person. In other words, the same person can play multiple roles and/or multiple people can play the same role.

Business domain expert

You absolutely cannot develop a good object model, and subsequently a good O-O system, without domain knowledge. Rapid modeling sessions are filled with questions, clarifications, issues, and definitions. These are essential to finding the right objects for your business and can only be gotten from an expert in the end users' needs, industry directions, and problem areas. A requirements document can help here, but is no substitute for an expert in the room.

Of course, the personality, communication abilities, and receptiveness of the expert can have vast effects on the success of the modeling. I vividly remember one modeling session where the expert brought in to support the modeling sessions really took to the concepts and techniques of what we were doing. By the end of the second week, he was even postulating good O-O designs himself and asking me about their pros and cons. This was at least partially responsible for the modeling effort being completed for the electronic tendering portion of the project in two weeks instead of the six weeks that had been scheduled.

One good characteristic of a domain expert is that she can ignore some amount of detail, especially in the early modeling stages, in order to firm up the object model. Focusing on too much detail can paralyze the group.

Object technology mentor

Just as you can't develop a successful O-O system without domain knowledge, you can't develop what I would call a successful O-O system[*] without object technology knowledge. There is no book or week class that produce in someone who can recognize a good object when she smells it. Read the previous sentence again. I have seen many projects fail on the premise that they can get the C++ compiler to stop complaining or that they read an O-O book and it was intuitively obvious. These are usually followed by "...and I've always done that." Of course, what they end up with is a large project with 12 classes, with names such as MainCode. They then complain about the lack of reuse and lowered maintenance costs and oversell of the technology. You cannot develop a good object model—your most important O-O software asset—without object technology expertise.

Object technology experts are also required to develop a good object model.

------

[*]I define success as "delivered on time and within budget." I would also add "and contributing reusable componentry while lowering maintenance costs."

Architect

Architects are needed on any system development to own and control the contracts between subsystems.

Have your most highly skilled people working on your key classes and the management of the relationships between subsystems. The architecture of an O-O system consists of:

- ◆ **Contracts between subsystems.** Contracts define the interface between subsystems and classes. This interface needs to be controlled, so that clients can treat the subsystem and classes as black boxes, ignoring the implementation details. This allows them to focus on the complexity of the part of the system they are responsible for.

- ◆ **Key classes that span subsystems.** There will normally be a few classes that are pervasive across your business. In retail, the Store and Person classes are examples. These classes can be owned by the architects, in a similar way that subsystem technical leads own the key classes within the subsystem. For example, the Sales subsystem key classes might include SalesTransaction and Tender.

Grow your team

Start with a small team, growing members into key roles, such as architects.

Start with less than six people (rule of thumb) for your kickoff phase, which runs between three to six months (see Fig. 3.3). Bring in O-O and domain expertise if necessary. Use these people to seed your expanding project team as technical leads and architects. They will generally be the most knowledgeable in object technology and the domain as you bring on new people.

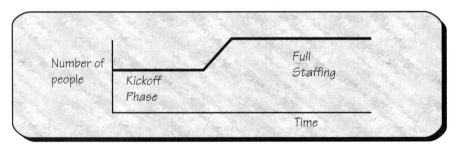

Figure 3.3. Growing your team over time.

Set up an apprentice or mentoring program at your company. This is extremely important. At the 1994 Workshop on Object-Oriented Design (WOOD), the consensus of many of the best O-O minds in the industry, was that the best way to develop good O-O people is to have them around good O-O people. "Cook books" can grow journeymen, but gurus need mentoring. And mentoring is the fastest way to move your people along the learning curve to good O-O development.

You may want to go so far as to assign mentors to particular people. In any case, you want to allow time for mentoring. It takes extra time in the short run but pays back dividends in time savings later.

Make sure that you list and fill team expertise requirements. Make a list of what expertise you need on your project. As you interview and hire people, check their expertise against your list. Make sure you fill all required categories. For example, if you need Smalltalk, Windows, RDB, and GUI expertise, use this list to drive your interview screening.

The learning curve

My rule of thumb is that it takes three to six months for someone to reach the point where she can work relatively independently and develop good models and designs. These "journeymen" still need an O-O guru to step in occasionally and help them with a point that is causing problems and to review their work periodically.

It takes another three to six months for someone to reach the point where she can drive an O-O effort. This step requires that she can not only develop good O-O systems, but can explain why decisions are made. This is much more difficult to do.

All these estimates assume full-time focus on O-O development and some O-O expertise is available during these periods to mentor the team.

Measure to focus mentoring

Collect metrics on your design as you go, watching for anomalies that flag developers who need additional mentoring. The sooner they get more on-the-job mentoring, the faster you'll be able to deliver high-quality O-O

Use design quality measurements to focus mentoring.

systems. See Lorenz (1994) for an in-depth discussion of O-O metrics. I would suggest the following as a minimum set of O-O metrics:

- ◆ **Method size.** Use the number of message sends to measure method sizes. In general, smaller is better. Averages over 12 message sends per method in a model class or 18 message sends per method in a view class can indicate the need for more mentoring.

- ◆ **Class size.** Focus on the number of public methods to measure class size. Again, in general, smaller is better. Large numbers of methods indicate too much responsibility in one class. Smaller classes tend to be more reusable. They also stick to doing one thing well.

- ◆ **Method overrides.** Subclassing should be by specialization. This means that the normal case is for subclasses that are "kinds of" their superclasses to add a few new methods. When a class overrides a number of superclass methods, it is indicative of a misplaced class in the inheritance hierarchy. Extensions of methods, such as occurs when a superclass method is invoked followed by additional code, and template methods, such as those designed in frameworks to be filled in by subclasses, do not count as overrides.

Hatteras Software has a product called OOMetric™ that measures the quality of your O-O designs.

Use creative education

Learning opportunities come in different flavors. Construct a set of educational offerings for your team:

- ◆ **Follow a roadmap.** Most O-O projects focus initially and primarily on language issues. This is the reverse of the recommended course to follow. Based on your requirements, you should (in this order):

→ Choose a methodology that conceptually covers your analysis and design needs and scales well

→ Choose a CASE tool that supports the chosen methodology

→ Choose a language that supports your design and implementation needs

→ Choose tools to support the chosen language based on your requirements.

♦ **Use a mentoring center.** It is pretty much universally agreed that the best way to learn something is to submerge yourself in it. If you're trying to learn to speak Japanese, this means you live in Japan for awhile; if you're trying to learn to use object technology effectively, you live at a mentoring center for awhile. In the case of O-O, "awhile" is at least a few weeks.

Mentoring centers provide the fastest way to grow O-O expertise in your organization.

What a mentoring center does is essentially put you on the fast track up the learning curve, by internalizing good modeling and design through numerous interactions with experienced O-O developers. If you need specialized expertise, whether it's GUIs or tools or design techniques, the expertise is readily available.

The best part about a mentoring center is that you get your real work done instead of working on a classroom application.

♦ **Use on-the-job training (OJT).** I've had people laugh at me for suggesting this point, which is surprising to me since I consider it to be obvious and common sense. If you are going to model the retail business, send some people into a local store to work as salespeople for awhile. The same goes for financial (local bank clerk), insurance (accompany a claims adjustor), and telephony (telephone sales) industries. The two most important assets in rapid modeling sessions are object technology and domain expertise. OJT gets some of the domain expertise in your people rapidly.

Measure your maturity

Evaluate your organization's maturity in using object technology (OT) to develop software. After performing this self-evaluation, you will be able to evaluate where your organization is today and prepare action plans for how to make further progress.

This kind of evaluation is useful on a periodic basis, comparing previous evaluations in order to continuously update current and future activities to maintain progress toward more effective use of the technology. You should expect differing levels of maturity in different categories; you do not give an overall rating. Also expect that different parts of your organization will be at different levels of maturity at any one time. Each independent organization can use this evaluation to prepare custom action plans.

Levels of maturity

Different terms are used for the different levels of maturity in using a technology. For this evaluation, we will use:

- **Awareness.** No use of OT in the organization

- **Trial use.** Experimenting with OT, but no formal use

- **Adoption.** Early use of OT in some areas

- **Institutionalization.** OT is the standard for the organization

- **Optimization.** State of the art use of OT throughout the organization

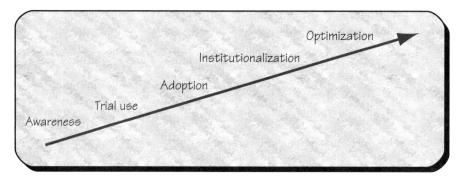

Figure 3.4. Increasing maturity levels.

These levels follow a progression for each measurement category, as shown in Figure 3.4.

Maturity categories

Fill in the following tables to evaluate your organization's maturity in using object technology. For each row, check the evaluation level that most closely matches a description of your organization. Once the evaluation is complete, develop a custom action plan for moving to the next level in each of the categories.

Literacy

Literacy has to do with the developer's shift to a new way of thinking about software development (Table 3.1).

Table 3.1. Literacy maturity form.

Awareness	Trial use	Adoption	Institutionalization	Optimization
Have heard about paradigm shift	Frustrated trying to understand paradigm	Rote use of the paradigm	Paradigm truly internalized	Making paradigm improvements
X	X	X	X	X
Have to-do list item to get education	Self education	Occasional formal education	Regularly scheduled formal education	Recommending education to others
X	X	X	X	X
Continuous mentoring required	Mentor required	Mentor needed	Providing own mentors	Providing mentors to other groups
X	X	X	X	X
Beginner	Novice	Journeyman	Expert	Guru
X	X	X	X	X
Not involved with conferences	Read conference proceedings	Attend conferences	Participate in conferences	Lead conferences
X	X	X	X	X
Never read articles	Seldom read articles	Occasionally read articles	Regularly read articles	Write articles
X	X	X	X	X

Process

Process looks at the development process used and what project controls are in place for that process (Table 3.2).

Table 3.2. Process maturity form.

Awareness	Trial use	Adoption	Institutionalization	Optimization
Have read about iterating	Limited trial use of iterations	Mechanically following iterative process from a book	Iterations understood and effective	Improving iterative process itself
X	X	X	X	X
Think about prototyping, but no time spent on it	Trial attempts at prototyping	Prototyping is part of the development process	Prototyping frequently occurs	Prototyping expected and occurs regularly
X	X	X	X	X
No metrics used	Ad hoc measurements	Measurements collected	Measurements used in scheduling	Metrics used to adapt schedules and designs
X	X	X	X	X
No reuse	Reuse actively encouraged	Reuse part of development process	Reuse is planned for	Reuse actually occurs
X	X	X	X	X

Methodology

Methodology examines the development steps followed (Table 3.3).

Table 3.3. Methodology maturity form.

Awareness	Trial use	Adoption	Institutionalization	Optimization
No O-O methodology used	Methodologies examined	Methodology officially chosen	Methodology followed	Methodology improved
X	X	X	X	X
No O-O tool s used	Tools examined	Tools chosen	Tool suite used	Integrated tool suite used
X	X	X	X	X
No O-O–specific documentation	Ad hoc documentation	Published documentation standards	Well-documented product assets	Documentation generated by tools
X	X	X	X	X
Copy and paste reuse	Locally specializing, searching, creating parts	Reusing parts across organization	Reusing designs	Code generation and reengineering
X	X	X	X	X

Assets

Assets are the product parts: people, designs, components, and documentation (Table 3.4).

Table 3.4. Asset maturity form.

Awareness	Trial use	Adoption	Institutionalization	Optimization
Monolithic code	Some classes in library	Reusable classes	Frameworks	Extensive parts across organization
X	X	X	X	X
Ad hoc product development	Some object model analysis attempted	Object modeling used	Object model required for all areas	Object model improved and extended
X	X	X	X	X
Industry standards known	Industry standards researched	Industry standard enablement planned	Industry standards required	Industry standards set
X	X	X	X	X
People are isolated	People's skills are locally recognized	People in demand inside company	People recognized outside company	People recognized across industry
X	X	X	X	X

The time to move between levels will vary greatly from situation to situation. An effective way to ensure continued progress is through periodic measurements, such as this evaluation exercise.

Run a pilot

A relatively small pilot project with a small team allows you to:

♦ **Build success.** Nothing breeds success like success. This applies both to team members, who gain confidence in tackling a new realm of software development, and management, which gets something solid to support instead of the usual pitch with nothing behind it.

- ◆ **Establish methodology, tools, process.** Many O-O projects are the first in their area and/or their company. It helps to have a small effort to prepare the way for future efforts by choosing the methodology, tools to support that methodology, and gain experience in the techniques for O-O development.

- ◆ **Mentor the core team.** You need to grow project members that can fill important roles, like object model architects. These roles are often initially filled by consultants from outside the group. Over time, your people will be able to fill these roles, but it takes time. A pilot gives them some of this time in a smaller, less threatening situation.

These will all contribute towards a faster product delivery by laying the groundwork early.

Remove constraints

Equipment

Your people are your most valuable asset. And their most valuable asset is their time. You do not want to waste precious seconds on a continuous basis while they wait on the computer to swap to/from disk, get information from a database, or any of the other constraints that may slow them down. Some of these are unavoidable or are too expensive to deal with, but you should opt for spending a few more dollars on a faster processor or more memory to speed up your development effort. Over time, you will get a good return on the investment.

Interruptions

Meetings, phone calls, pitches to customers, in-baskets full of mail, and all the other interruptions in your developers' time detract from the overall goal of delivering on time and within budget. You need to keep in mind the rule of thumb that it takes 20 minutes[†] to really get back to making good progress on the effort at hand. Again, view your developers' time as a precious resource—don't waste it on "busy work." It is easy to fill the day with relatively unimportant things. How many times have you heard people say "I get more done in the last hour of work, after everyone's gone and the phone quits ringing, than I do the whole rest of the day?"

Project patterns

Coplien (1994) talks about using patterns for organizational decisions, to allow the project to progress faster and have a higher probability of success. In this section, I'll discuss some of the project patterns that we reuse on our O-O projects.

- ◆ **Architected decomposition.** In this pattern, a small team creates the initial object model core with the key classes and subsystems identified and assigned contracts. Reaching this point allows the project to break up into multiple subsystem teams with one or two architects managing the documented interfaces between the subsystems.

- ◆ **Seamless teams.** In this pattern, the same team works on many phases of the project, instead of having separate analysts, designers, and programmers. This has been shown to be especially effective in O-O system development, where domain knowledge and terminology take on added value since they more directly correspond to the implementation details.

- ◆ **Iterative process.** This is discussed elsewhere in this book as well as in Lorenz (1993). This pattern facilitates rapid customer feed-

---

[†]Let's not debate the exact number. It may be 15 or 25 minutes. The point is that valuable time is lost.

back by regularly involving them in the on-going development. This allows for smaller corrections to be made multiple times over the life of the project without disruption the overall effort.

♦ **Mentoring culture.** A mentoring culture pattern has experienced O-O developers working with novice O-O developers. Something like this is fairly normal on most projects. The difference with this pattern is the emphasis on truly working with the other team members, much as a consultant works with customers or a teacher works with students. Traditionally, the team is much more competitive. This pattern implies that each member actively works at learning from all other members (i.e., no turf wars).

♦ **Sow seeds.** This successful pattern starts the modeling team out with a few people, who move along the learning curve quickly. They then become the "seeds" for other small teams as the overall project grows in staff size. My rule of thumb is that each team has at least one O-O and domain-knowledgeable person in it from the initial team. The original team also provides the architect(s) for the project.

♦ **Encapsulate authority.** Much as good O-O systems have self-managing objects, good O-O projects have self-managing subsystem teams. Seed the team with a technical lead who was a part of the initial modeling effort, where she gained domain knowledge as well as experience in high-quality object modeling and design.

♦ **Ignore constraints initially.** This process pattern allows for a more accurate model of the business domain, since the team largely ignores implementation details such as database schemas and performance constraints. Our early analysis guideline is to "assume unlimited resources." I know many cringe at this statement, but it has helped speed up the modeling effort by keeping the team focused on the business domain essentials long enough to get a good model base. There is plenty of time later to focus on detailed implementation. Besides, my experience has been that performance issues are not where people postulate they will be, so why chase problems that may not exist?‡

Domain experts are required to develop a good object model.

---

‡Certainly, for known performance risks you should prototype possible solutions early in the effort. My experience for projects with tight performance requirements is that these should still not drive the early efforts.

Chapter **4**

CASE Tools

Computer-aided software engineering (CASE) tools have historically provided a relatively small return on the investment. But not to worry. This has mostly occurred due to the limitations of structured techniques, which have dominated the CASE world to date. Object technology benefits carry over into CASE tools as well.

In the past, there was a wall between phases of a project, as shown in Figure 4.1. This wall consisted at its root of a difference in how the work was being done. This difference caused a nonautomatable gap to occur between phases such as analysis and design. This inhibits effective communication between team members and development phases.

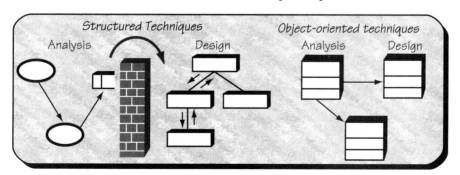

Figure 4.1. Breaking down the phase barrier.

Object technology removes the activity gaps for CASE tools

With O-O techniques, the gap disappears. You work with the same objects in the different phases, changing your focus and the number of details as you go. This greatly reduces the burden on CASE tools, since no translation is required.

Code generation

It is imperative to carry any information gathered during your analysis and design into later efforts on the project. Any tool(s) you choose should sup-

```
Application create: #InventoryManagement with:
        (#( CommonApplicationFramework )
        collect: [:each | Smalltalk at: each ifAbsent: [
        self error: 'Not all of the prerequisites are loaded']])!

InventoryManagement becomeDefault!

Object subclass: #InvInventory
        instanceVariableNames: 'products'
        classVariableNames: ''
        poolDictionaries: '' !




InvInventory comment: 'Inventory is the current stock of Products in
U-Call-Us"s Warehouse. It is essentially a smart container.'!

!InvInventory class publicMethods !

placeOrderFor: anAmount
"
!!


...

InventoryManagement loaded!
```

Figure 4.2. Example of generated code for VisualAge Team.

port generation of code skeletons that include the design as well as commentary information forward. (Fig. 4.2).

This means that:

♦ Subsystems become applications in Envy or packages in Team/V.

♦ Contracts become categories for their related classes.

♦ Comments become true comments in the browser.

♦ Private and public method information carries over to the browser.

Reengineering

If you are rapidly moving between modeling and prototyping, as I have recommended, then you need tool(s) that support this movement between activities. One facet of this requirement is the ability to synchronize the information in your model with the information in your development environment.

Pulling information out of a development environment and object model and being able to selectively update your model and/or your development environment so that the two match each other is what I am calling *reengineering*.

Tools are necessary to support a rapid movement between modeling and prototyping.

Online documentation

All information about subsystems, classes, responsibilities (instance and class methods), state data (instance and class variables), issues, and scenario scripts should be captured into tool(s). This information should be viewable online as well as printable as hardcopy in various layouts as specified by the user. (See Figs. 4.3 through 4.6.)

Information entered in your CASE tools should be available for your design specifications.

Basic mail-order sale
- This script details our phone order-taking procedures from customers
InterfaceSubsystem requests customerFor: aPhoneNumber from **Company**
      Company asks hasPhoneNumber: aPhoneNumber from **Person**
      script: New customer
      script: Customer information updates
      branch: Bad credit record
InterfaceSubsystem requests productNumbered: aNumber from **Inventory**

Figure 4.3. Sample script output from HOMSuite.

Product
An Item in the Inventory that a Customer can order.

    Owner   nil
    Subsystem   Stocking
    Superclass   Object (A)
    Subclasses
    Contracts and associated Responsibilities
        Maintain inventory levels
    Public responsibilities
        *price
    Instance state data
        number

Figure 4.4. Sample class documentation output from HOMSuite.

Standard formats

A proposed standard format for CASE tools is called *CASE Data Interchange Format* (CDIF). If possible, you should use tools that will import and export to and from CDIF. This will give you the flexibility to move between tools easily instead of being locked into one vendor and tool suite.

```
    \par \pard\plain \s5\f1\fs36\cf0\b\ql\sb144\sa72\brdrt\keep\keepn\pagebb
Overview
\par \pard\plain \s0\cf0\sb144 \fi720 \ql
This document describes the system object model,
which includes subsystems, contracts, classes, and scripts.
\par \pard\plain \s5\f1\fs36\cf0\b\ql\sb144\sa72\brdrt\keep\keepn\pagebb
Object Model
\par \pard\plain \s0\cf0\sb144 \fi720 \ql
\par \pard\plain \s5\f1\fs32\cf0\sb216\sa72\ql\b\i
Object model objects
\par \pard\plain \s0\cf0\sb144 \fi720 \ql
\par \pard\plain \s5\f1\fs28\cf0\sb216\sa72\ql\b\i
Company
\par \pard\plain \s0\cf0\sb144 \fi720 \ql
Our business "The Hatteras Electronics Boutique"
\par \pard\plain \s0\cf0\sb144 \ri576 \ql \b Owner
\par \pard\plain \s0\cf0\sb72 \ri720 \ql nil
\par \pard\plain \s0\cf0\sb144 \ri576 \ql \b Subsystem
\par \pard\plain \s0\cf0\sb72 \ri720 \ql System
\par \pard\plain \s0\cf0\sb144 \ri576 \ql \b Superclass
\par \pard\plain \s0\cf0\sb72 \ri720 \ql Object A)
\par \pard\plain \s0\cf0\sb144 \ri576 \ql \b Subclasses
\par \pard\plain \s0\cf0\sb72 \ri720 \ql
```

Figure 4.5. Sample Rich Text Format (RTF) output from HOMSuite.

Development tools

This section deals with the myriad topics surrounding the pragmatics of the development effort, such as group development support and on-line help.

Leveraging groupware

Painless trial and error

Tools such as Envy and Team/V allow you to try things out, knowing that you can easily go back to a different state by simply reloading another version of the software.

This frees you up even more than before to try several possibilities. One way we have done this in Team/V is to rename a package, thereby severing the relationship to the package file on disk while retaining the starting version of the software. You can then make whatever changes you want and even commit the package (to another file on disk) without affecting the mainstream development. You can then later decide to accept or abandon the redesign. Of course, in the meantime, you have a double maintenance effort to keep the two candidate designs in sync.

This can also help if you need to perform regression testing for versions of your software that are still out in the field. You can load a release based on a configuration map (for Envy) or build script (for Team/V).

On-line design reviews

A group support tool such as Envy can be used to support design reviews without the need for additional meetings. Sridhar (1992) discusses some of the techniques that have been used to hold on-line design reviews by leveraging Envy. What you can do is have people, at their leisure and without holding a formal meeting, browse the portion of the system to be reviewed and give direct feedback through the browser. This feedback can take a couple of forms. One is by adding commentary to the methods, classes, and/or applications. Another is by creating a scratch edition and redesigning a portion to show how you would have improved the design. The reviewee can then incorporate any feedback by merely getting onto Envy at her leisure and deciding what she wants to do with the comments and suggested code changes. The owner is the only person who can version any changes and so retains control throughout the review.

You can do similar reviews through Team/V by creating branches off of a revision or a release of a package.

Test cases

Envy and Team/V let you extend a class in a separate application or package respectively. You may want to separate your test case code into appropriately named packages, such as *<package name> test cases.*

Surrounding efforts

On-line help

Creating on-line help can be time-consuming. Fortunately, WYSIWYG tools are helping more (pun intended). What we are doing for our Smalltalk projects is to provide the bulk of the documentation on-line, with a small installation/getting started manual in hardcopy.

In our user's manual, we put a lot of graphics from our products, with regions on the bitmaps set up as buttons that activate definition popup dialogs or bring up another window, much as would happen in the product. In this way, the user can interact with a helpful version of the product UI, exploring its capabilities in parallel with the real product.

Noteworthy products

RoboHelp™ from Blue Sky Software is the best help development product for Windows™ that I've found. It is built on top of Word™. It allows for direct action manipulation of hyperlinkages, graphics, indexes, and all the other features a good help should have.

Hyperwise™ from IBM is a newer product that has many, but not all, the features of RoboHelp. Hyperwise's appeal to my company is that it will generate help files for OS/2™ as well as Windows. Since my company delivers products on multiple platforms, including OS/2 and Windows, this saves us a great deal of effort in recreating help in two formats.

Graphical methodology support

Visio™ from ShapeWare is a wonderful drawing tool for Windows. It offers palettes of smart shapes, including an Advanced Software package that includes many major O-O notations. Hatteras Software has developed some extensions to support RDD notations, including contracts and subsystems. We use subsystem sheets to create levels of detail, which can be traversed by double-clicking within a subsystem. Using Visio this way, along with our HOMSuite modeling tool, we have a very inexpensive O-O CASE set of tools that have been very effective in our Smalltalk projects.

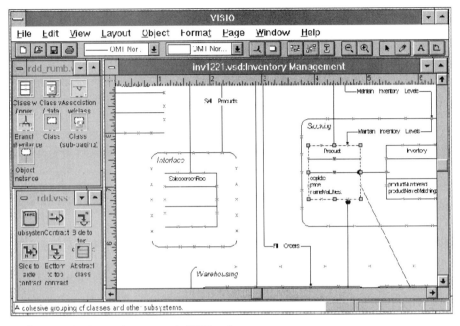

Figure 4.6. Visio with our extended RDD palette.

Using a GUI builder

The main purpose of this section is to give you some tips on how to make effective use of some GUI builders that relate to Smalltalk development. This section will not teach you to use a particular GUI builder, and it will not focus on their capabilities, since that type of information will be quickly out of date and not as useful.

In general, a GUI builder is an absolute necessity. Do not waste your development time creating views by hand, unless you need custom widgets. Even then, create any custom widgets so that they work with existing GUI builders. The GUI is the most volatile portion of your system. You want to minimize the amount of effort to develop and maintain it. You also want to make it easy to change, since you don't want to resist improvements to the GUI suggested by your end users.

Division of responsibility

A key point in O-O development that often causes groups to stumble is where to draw the line of doing work in the view versus its collaborating model objects. The choices of where to draw these divisions of responsibility across the model and view objects is very important. Some guidelines include:

Dividing lines between the model and the view are critical to achieving higher levels of reuse and less maintenance.

♦ **Related model actions.** If you have a case where multiple actions are supposed to always take place together, you should put these behaviors in the model objects' methods. This will ensure that the model does not get in an illegal state as well as saving effort for all future clients of this service.

For example, suppose you wanted to make sure that Inventory was depleted whenever a sale took place and that this fact was logged to disk. The view objects should not be involved in this activity. Model objects should take care of their own business to ensure their state is always valid.

In this example, the SalesLineItem could ask the InventoryItem to deplete its amountOnHand and the InventoryItem could log this action. Any of these events could use the dependency mechanism to notify interested GUI view objects of the state change so that it could be reflected on the screen.

♦ **Presentation.** The way that something is presented can vary greatly. Perhaps icons are used with drag-and-drop capabilities, multimedia voice input and video output, listboxes, single document interface, and so on. The many ways that information is presented and interacted with are all the domain of the view objects. The relatively stable model should remain independent of the view. Views should be pluggable.

♦ **Validation.** There are multiple types of validation:

→ *Field format.* This deals with the types of characters being entered, such as integers or alphabetic, and the size of fields. This is the responsibility of the view objects, such as windows and dialogs.

→ *Semantic relationships.* This deals with the business rules between the model objects' state. A value entered on the UI may relate to other model objects, whether that should be valid or not. This is the responsibility of the model objects. For example, if adding a Transaction to a ClientAccount means that the Account balance should be updated, this responsibility belongs with the Account model objects.

There are a number of reasons for this allocation. The most important reasons relate to reuse and integrity. Multiple view objects can reuse the services of the model objects, whereas validation put in another view may not be available or known about. The model integrity can only be maintained when it is maintained by the model itself. Otherwise, the first view object developer that forgets to enforce some business rule will corrupt your model state.

Pay attention to what logic you put into view objects. They should stick to presentation issues, not business logic. Your model should be built so that it ensures its state. Putting the logic in the model also provides reuse for other view builders.

GUI builder guidelines

The following general guidelines will help you effectively use any GUI builder:

♦ **Explicitly name all parts.** Most GUI builders generate a default name for your UI components. They are generic names such as *button1* or *listbox2*. Make sure you give your components meaningful names to make the code more readable.

♦ **Use composite parts.** Composite parts are groupings of UI controls with their associated actions upon certain events, plus possibly some model objects and logic underneath.

  By creating and reusing composite parts, you get a more consistent UI in a shorter period of time. Have your GUI framework builder be responsible for building composite parts for the project team.

Groups of UI widgets can be reused, providing consistency and speeding up the UI development.

♦ **Use a single document interface (SDI).** This type of interface is more closely aligned with an O-O system, since it focuses a window on one primary object and its associated objects. Multidocument interfaces (MDI), which have clipped child windows that share one menu bar, are less flexible relative to today's drag-and-drop O-O interfaces.

WindowBuilder Pro™

WindowBuilder Pro is a GUI builder from ObjectShare that works with different versions of Smalltalk/V™ from Digitalk (see Fig. 4.7).

  An interesting productivity feature is the ability to create "composite" objects. The user is able to group her own sets of GUI widgets into a higher-level reusable widget. This really speeds up the effort and helps standardize the GUI across the project.

  The clipboard is also readily available. It is very fast through the menu (and even faster through the keyboard) to copy and paste widgets.

WindowBuilder Pro gives you a designed place to get control of the GUI events during the creation of a window or dialog. An initWindow method of your design is invoked before the window is actually opened. This allows you to initialize control contents, for example.

Referencing WindowBuilder Pro widgets is a matter of using their paneNamed: method. You can remove yourself one layer from the implementation details by defining a set of accessing methods such as:

xyzPane

^(self paneNamed: 'xyz')

This technique also makes it easy to locate references to the UI widget, since local senders of a method selector can be requested via the browsers.

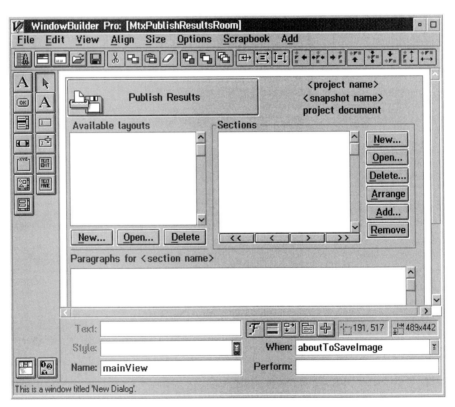

Figure 4.7. Example use of WindowBuilder Pro.

Overall, WindowBuilder Pro is a great value for the money. Object-Share is coming out with more widgets for their palette, including business graphics and spreadsheets.

VisualWorks™

VisualWorks is ParcPlace's GUI-building tool suite that works with Object-Works/Smalltalk™. VisualWorks' forte is portability. The GUI builder part of the product even allows you to choose the look and feel of the target platform, in Figure 4.8 OS/2 CUA.

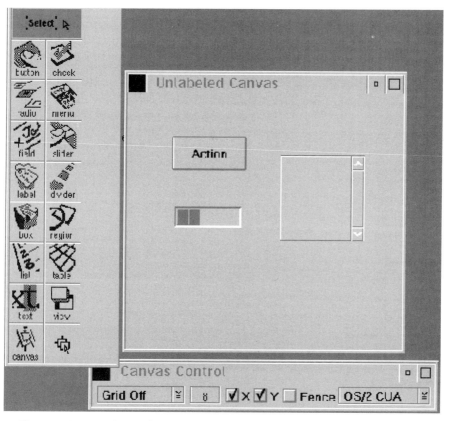

Figure 4.8. Example use of VisualWorks.

VisualAge™

VisualAge is IBM's graphical development tools that work on top of IBM Smalltalk™ in team and standalone environments. Communication classes, such as TCP/IP, and database classes, such as DB2, are available.

VisualAge makes it extremely easy to connect windows to database fields, since it provides the visual facilities to define a basic broker-type mapping between fields and GUI widgets. This is similar to what you can do with 4GL visual tools and is fine for an ad hoc application. But it does not get you long-term reuse, extensibility, or maintainability. Be careful to resist the temptation to cut out the model layer for your strategic applications!

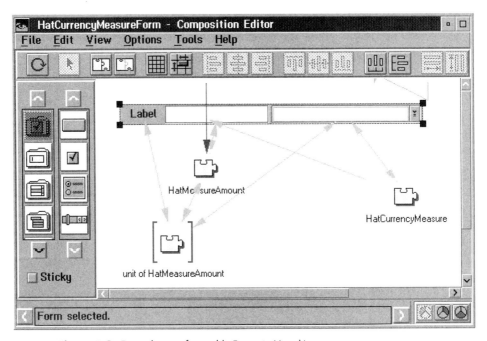

Figure 4.9. Example use of reusable Forms in VisualAge.

VisualAge also makes it easy to put a lot in one visual part. My rule of thumb is that one visual part contains at most one window and its related dialogs.* I then use variables to communicate between visual parts.

Similar to composite objects in WindowBuilder Pro, VisualAge allows you to create **Forms**, which are composed of groupings of basic parts and their connections. For example, I created a **CurrencyForm** part, which I can then use in multiple applications (see Fig. 4.9). Windows merely includes the **CurrencyForm** part of the palette, and it handles math expressions between different types of currencies for them.

IBM is fostering a parts community for VisualAge through their Object Connection program, so I would expect a continuous stream of new parts to become available for their palettes.

Configuration management

Irrespective of whether you use object technology in your projects or not, you need to insure yourself against disaster. Back up your project information and store it off-site on a regular basis. No tool will be able to totally avoid disasters[†] and you cannot afford to lose days of work of multiple highly paid expert software developers.

Working in groups

Smalltalk provides a wonderful development environment. It is also a single-user environment. No real commercial project can afford to be without

---

*Of course, you can have visual parts that don't have views! This allows for visual programming of connections for model objects that work together.

[†]See Lorenz (Oct 1994) for details of how to recover from a crash.

group support. I will talk about using two different Smalltalk groupware tools in this section.

Envy

Envy/Developer is a multi-user development environment for Smalltalk. The good news is that Envy is the best Smalltalk group development tool for large projects that I know of. The bad news is that Envy's UI needs improvement.

Envy divides the effort into *applications*, which we equate with sub-systems. Envy works across a local area network (LAN), saving changes in realtime to the server database. Changes come in the form of *editions* and *versions*. An edition is a component that is still being worked on. A version is an edition that has been released for public consumption and can no longer be directly changed (although another edition of it may be created).

If the LAN is down, you are dead in the water with Envy, so it is very important that you have reliable power sources. I would recommend your own battery backup for power outages. I would also recommend a support contract, as I have seen projects need to use this online support to recover from corrupted Envy databases.

Application choices

We use applications to represent the subsystems in our architecture. We don't use subapplications very often, so subsystems within subsystems map to applications in Envy.

Team/V

Team/V is a multi-user development environment for Smalltalk/V. Team/V breaks the effort into *packages*, which we again equate with subsystems. It uses the PVCS™ library system for storage of packages.

Package choices

We have found it useful to define packages along the lines of a functional piece of the system, for the mainstream application as well as support subsystems. We have also found it useful to break up the UI into packages along the lines of its design.

For example, we make a package for a window and all its related dialogs. We make a separate package for the model classes in a particular subsystem.

Chapter 5

Higher levels of reuse

A KEY TO FASTER delivery of software systems is *reuse*. This often-quoted concept is often missing from systems being built today. Most of the stumbling blocks are organizational rather than technical.

The organization needs to be willing to include reuse in its performance review process, provide incentives for reuse, foster a culture of reuse rather than reinvention, remove legal constraints as much as possible to make componentry available, and dedicate resources for a cross-project componentry department and to support a reuse library.

Technically, tools to help find components to reuse and a reuse library certification process need to be defined.

This section of the book will discuss various ways you can enhance reuse, which is an essential part of rapid software development.

Reuse is <u>the</u> single most effective means to achieve faster software development.

A reuse process

Every project should identify some model objects to contribute to the company's reuse library.

Reuse should be an intrinsic part of all phases of your development (Fig. 5.1). During the early phases, you focus on planning to reuse existing componentry as well as planning to contribute new components to the reuse library. These plans should be documented in the appropriate specifications for the project.

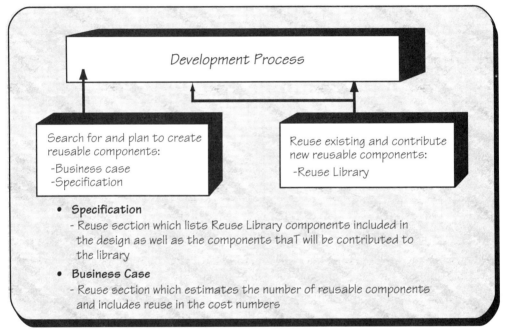

Figure 5.1. Including reuse in your development process.

During the actual development, you fulfill this plan, measuring your actual performance relative to reuse. In choosing candidate classes and subsystems to contribute to the reuse library, focus on the new and advanced features of your system under development. Candidate components include:

- ◆ For a telephony project: Call class, CallFeatures subsystem (call waiting, call forwarding, ...)

- ◆ For a retail project: Accounting subsystem, SalesTransaction class, ActivityLog class

- ◆ For an inventory project: InventoryItem class, Ordering subsystem

♦ For a banking project: ElectronicTendering subsystem, Account class

Domain overlap

The amount of reuse you can expect to achieve across multiple projects is partially determined by how related the business domains are among the projects.

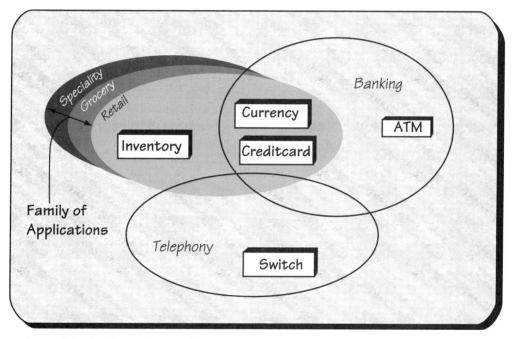

Figure 5.2. Overlapping business domains.

For example, if you have previously developed a product in the retail point of sale (POS) specialty domain, you will get more reuse for similar domains such as grocery stores than for vastly different domains such as telephony (see Fig. 5.2). Other domains, such as financial, may have partial overlap for areas such as electronic tendering for credit, debit, and smart cards.

Projects in the same family of applications as previous projects will be able to achieve the highest level of reuse.

Organize for reuse

In the section on the team, I mentioned a role of *class developer*. This implies
a direction for the organization to facilitate and manage reuse (see Fig. 5.3).

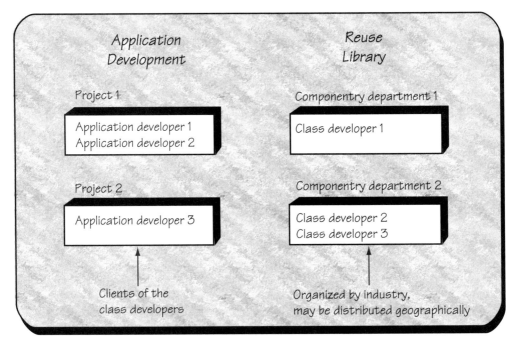

Figure 5.3. Reuse roles.

    Application developers are the customers of the class developers. Class
developers own the key business classes that have surfaced in previous
projects' reuse development process. This type of organization keeps parochial issues from creeping into generic reusable componentry. Lets face it—
when the pressures to get the product out come along, developers are going
to do whatever it takes, including putting in ad hoc changes. Also, you can
"bubble" requirements from multiple projects into the components in the
reuse library, making them more useful.

    Your best people should be class developers. This group should grow over
time if you are being successful in your reuse program. Application developer
groups should shrink over time and require relatively less skilled people.

Build for the second time

Plan a second (re)use for parts of your system during the first design. This forces you to deal with reuse issues very explicitly, and you end up with components that are more reusable from the first release.

While I worked at IBM, I was the technical lead of an O-O project to build a reuse support tool. It was named Reuse Support System (RSS) and was successfully released internally and featured in the book *Objects in Action* by Paul Harmon and David Taylor (Harmon, 1993). I was pleased to see that it has since been released as a product named ReDiscovery. Our design process included this technique. We kept future reuse plans in mind for a number of areas of the system, so that we did not end up with an ad hoc solution for our first release. For example, we kept mainframe searches in mind when designing how workstation searches would work. What resulted was a system that was more flexible in useful ways for future releases.

Keep logic in the model

O-O developers often draw the line between the UI and the model farther toward the model than is optimal for reuse (Fig. 5.4). I catch myself, even after all these years, putting too much functionality in the UI classes. It's easy to do in the heat of rapid functionality development.

It is very important to keep business logic in the model, not the view.

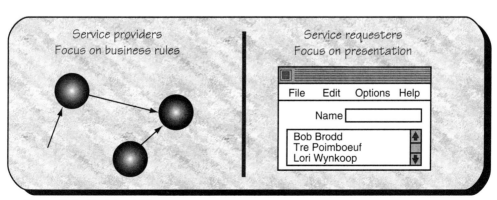

Figure 5.4. Model vs. UI focus.

For example, Figure 5.5 shows a piece of code as it was initially designed. The view class client of the Widget model class is performing work that is necessary to keep the model consistent. The model expects certain things to always be in place for the system to work. In this example, aWidget isn't supposed to exist without a name and a parent. The design relies on each and every client of Widget to create it properly. As soon as someone forgets, problems occur.

```
XyzView>>newWidget
    "return a new Widget to use"

    | newWidget |
    newWidget := Widget new.
    newWidget name: ( self paneNamed: 'name' ) contents.
    newWidget parent: self currentContainer.
    ^newWidget
```

Figure 5.5.

By rewriting the code as shown in Figure 5.6, there is added functionality in the model, which can be leveraged by all clients in the future.

There is another important benefit of these changes is that you end up with a more solid model class and overall product as well as reduced maintenance costs. This is due to the fact that there is one place where this functionality is handled, so you don't get developers introducing bugs into the system. If there is a needed change in the future, there is one place to change. It is not possible to forget about one of the places that repeat similar code that needs changing as well.

```
XyzView>>newWidget
    "return a new Widget to use"

    ^Widget named: ( self paneNamed: 'name' ) contents
            for: self currentContainer.

Widget class>>named: aString for: aContainer
    "return an instance of myself with its name and parent set"

    ^self new
        name: aString;
        parent: aContainer;
        yourself
```

Figure 5.6.

As shown in the redesigned code, the Widget class provides a public method named:for: to create instances of itself with the required initial state, using its private name: and parent: methods.

Granted, this is a simple example, but it illustrates the point of staying alert to where to draw the line in functionality.

Enhance searches

One of the technical issues to resolve is how to make it less expensive in time and effort for a developer to reuse an existing component than it is to reinvent a custom, ad hoc work of art. This requires:

◆ **A tool to allow searches of what's available.** Searches need to be flexible. Prompting for message selectors is not enough. You need tools that allow boolean expressions to be used to locate candidate components. For example, searches such as

(sort* or collate) and report*

should be supported.

One tool that goes a long way toward achieving this kind of flexibility is ReDiscovery™ from IBM.

◆ **Certification of reuse library components.** As I've stated before, there's only one thing worse than finding a bug in your code—finding a bug in someone else's code. If someone tries to reuse a component from the reuse library and gets burned by poor quality, she will not be easily tempted to come back and try again. Make sure the components have been rigorously tested beyond what you'd normally do for a single project.

◆ **Good documentation for the reuse library components.** People need to be able to quickly understand if a component meets their needs. This includes information such as:

➙ Summary of capabilities

→ Examples of usage

→ Restrictions

The documentation needs to be better than that done for components that are not in the reuse library.

Use frameworks

Framework[*] is one of those terms that is used a lot, is basically understood, and is often misused and misunderstood. I'm going to give multiple definitions, much as a dictionary might:

1. A set of prebuilt classes and methods that define the basic structure of some end user functions, leaving the application-specific details to be filled in by developers.

2. A portion of a software system that is designed to provide some useful services through refinement and extension by client developers.

3. At an implementation level, a set of classes that cooperate to achieve the goal of providing some functionality.

4. An implementation of a design pattern.

Frameworks can and should be one of the easiest ways to productive reuse. Understanding the framework largely determines how effective it is. Documentation is a large part of that understanding.

---

[*]There was an awful lot of valuable discussion of frameworks at WOOD this year in Utah. I'd like to acknowledge and thank the participants for indirectly helping me make this a better section of the book.

What to document

I'm including a sort of exhaustive list of possibilities you may want to document for a framework. Use the list to decide which ones you want to include or exclude.

- **Intent.** What is this framework for? What problems does it solve? What does it not address? This section should be an "executive summary" of the framework.

- **Decisions made and rationale.** What choices were made during the design? Why? What effects will this have on clients of the framework?

- **Rules to obey.** What are the intended uses of the parts of the framework? Conceptually, what are the correct and incorrect ways to (re)use the framework?

- **Dimensions of refinement.** What details are expected to be filled in by clients? What areas are not to be changed by clients? What areas can optionally be extended by clients?

- **Examples.** What are some typical sample uses of the framework? Which one should be looked at first? What are the best uses of the framework? How exactly was it used, step by step?

- **Structure.** What is the interface for the client? For the extender? The interrelationships should be shown in pictorial as well as textual form.

- **Logical design.** What does a graphical representation of the key design points look like?

- **Performance considerations.**

- **Test suite.** This should include a sample application.

- **Companion frameworks.** List other frameworks that work well with this one.

- **Support tools.**

- **Indexes.**

- **Sales pitch.**

- ◆ Theory of operation.
- ◆ **Sibling frameworks.** List other frameworks that compete with this one.
- ◆ **Dependent frameworks.**
- ◆ **Extension advice.**
- ◆ **Set of operating conditions.** What environment, class library, etc. is required to use this framework?

Modeling patterns

Modeling patterns are a promise of reuse. They are especially potent because the intent of the reuse is at a higher level than most reuse today. They are an abstraction of a design.

There are some debates raging about the definition of a *pattern*. For our purposes here, we'll use the following definition: A basic design rule that can be used to guide the development of frameworks.

Patterns are abstractions that evolve from anecdotal instances (idioms) related to the patterns. In other words, we notice a recurring theme in good designs. We postulate what the essence of that theme is and we end up documenting a pattern.

A key point to get the most out of patterns is to focus on the interface. As Gamma (1994) states,

> *[The] principle of reusable object-oriented design [is to] program to an interface, not an implementation. Avoid committing to a particular class, but instead commit only to an interface defined by an abstract class.*

Modeling idioms

An idiom is a particular instance of a pattern. Generally, the idioms come first, resulting in our noticing the pattern. It's sort of like discovering abstract classes as you build up your object model. For each of the patterns, I will give at least one example of its use (an idiom). I have seen these patterns of design on a number of projects and suggest you consider them for reuse on your project, saving you time and effort.

Object persistence

In this case, you would ideally like to use an object database (ODB) to encapsulate most of the details for managing persistent objects. However, many projects don't have this luxury since they must interact with an existing relational database (RDB) that is still being used by legacy systems. This is in keeping with the strategy of replacing portions of the existing business software in an evolutionary fashion, thereby controlling the amount of investment and risk at any one time.

This pattern has a **Proxy** object standing in for some persistent object that is not currently in memory (see Fig. 5.7). When a message is sent to the **Proxy**, it captures the **doesNotUnderstand** method and uses its **objectID** to send an **object**: message to the object **Registrar**. The persistent object can then be reinstantiated from disk and the Proxy can be replaced by the real object, such as through a **become**: message.

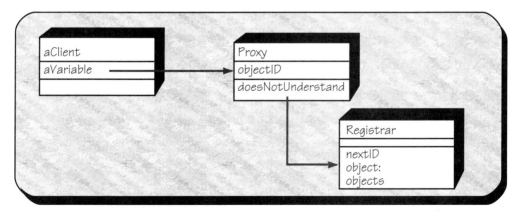

Figure 5.7. Basic structure of an idiom for a Proxy pattern.

Going the other direction, you must decide when objects will be replaced by their **Proxies**. This may be after some service is completed, when memory is low, when other events are bringing more objects into memory (which will involve the **Registrar**), and so on.

RDB Access

The mismatch between relational databases (RDBs) and O-O systems is a reality we will have to live with for many years. Certainly, using an object database (ODB) will alleviate the need for this pattern.

In this pattern, you have a layer of **Broker** objects between your business model objects and the database layer objects (Fig. 5.8). The **Broker** deals with the specifics of what fields in records are used to instantiate its specific type of model object, filling in the state data for the object. The database objectsinterface with the database management system (DBMS), such as through SQL queries. Various database schemas can be handled by the **Broker** layer. This pattern can be used in coordination with the *Object persistence* pattern.

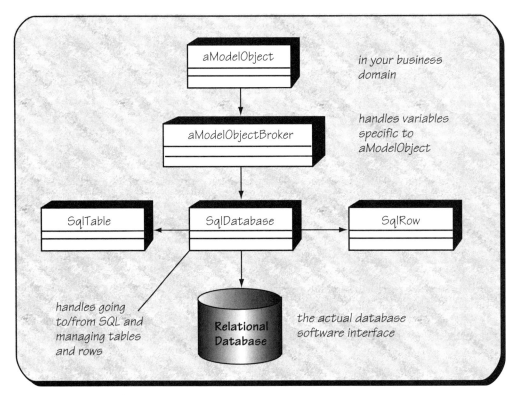

Figure 5.8. DB Broker pattern.

Let's look at an example idiom for **Customer** and **Address** model classes in Figures 5.9 and 5.10. The related **Broker** classes understand the record layout and how it relates to the state data for an instance of its related model object.

You may even want **Broker** frameworks for each variant of the DB storage.

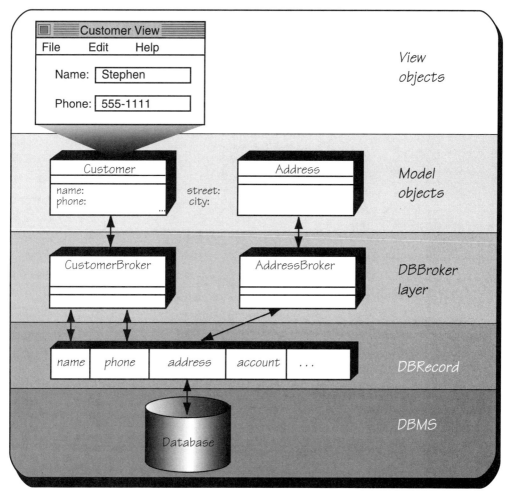

Figure 5.9. Example of Broker idiom.

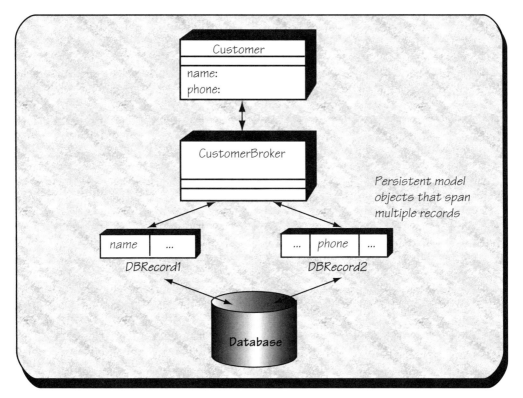

Figure 5.10. Alternative Broker idiom.

Roles

Most systems have a need for the same objects to play different roles in different scenarios. The most common example relates to people in the business model. Our initial model may contain **Manager**, **Clerk**, and **Customer** classes. That is all well and good, but the same **Person** can be all of the above at different times.

One way[†] to improve the model is to use **Roles** (see Fig. 5.11).

[†]Another way is through multiple inheritance, which I do not recommend. Besides the fact that Smalltalk does not support it, it has possible adverse side affects such as method lookup name collisions and a steeper learning curve.

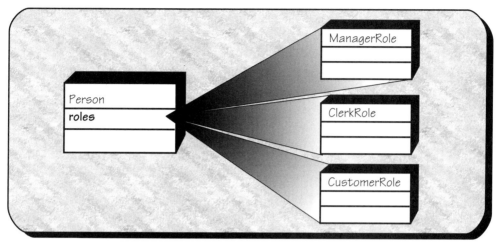

Figure 5.11. An example of the use of Roles.

Role objects can be used for a number of collaborations, including the filtering of system capabilities. The Person's currentRole can be used to find out what the Person is authorized to do. This in turn can affect what options appear on the different View objects' menus and other controls.

Alarms

This pattern provides for fault-tolerant event management. Objects register for notification at a certain time. An idiom is to have an AlarmClock that allows objects to give it a message selector, a time, and an object (Fig. 5.12). It then writes this information to disk and periodically checks its list of events. Whenever an event has passed its time, the AlarmClock sends the specified message to the object.

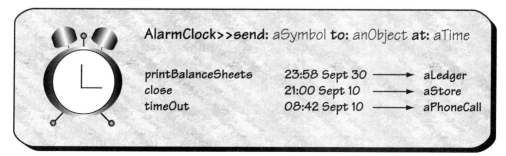

Figure 5.12. Using an AlarmClock pattern.

New types

Most projects need to be able to create new types of objects while in production.

A pattern I have seen a number of times is the desire on the part of end users to define new "types" of objects. What they are really after is a way to customize the behavior of some set of base types. In a development environment, you would handle this by creating a subclass specialization of the related type. However, this requires being able to create new "types" in the production environment at the customer site. The pattern is to build this flexibility by creating OptionTables for the objects, which allow the user to enter values that affect the behaviors of the model objects.

Figure 5.13 shows an example idiom in the retail industry, where new types of Tender are desired. What we did was to create what we called a TenderTable to maintain the initial state data values.

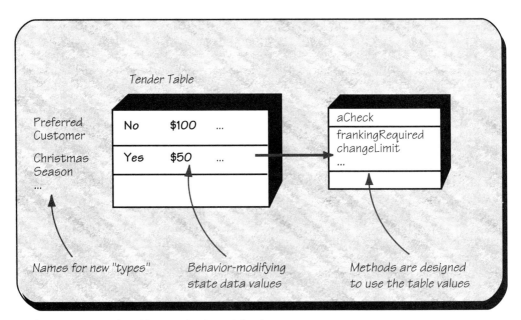

Figure 5.13. Tender table example of user-defined types.

We then used an initializeFrom: class method to create and load the state of a new instance, as shown in Figure 5.14.

> Check
>
> **initializeFrom:** aTenderTableRow
>   "load my state with a TenderTableRow values"
>   ^self new
>   frankingRequired: aTenderTableRow frankingRequired;
>   changeLimit: aTenderTableRow changeLimit;
>   ...
>   yourself

Figure 5.14. Initializing new types.

The **Check** class' methods use the state values from the table entry to decide how to behave.

Wrapper

Wrappers insulate the client classes from the details of the wrapper contents, managing the details of the interface to its contents.

An example idiom is where the wrapper contents is a portion of an existing non–O-O system (Fig. 5.15). The rest of the system does not need to know that the function-oriented world is out there and must be dealt with.

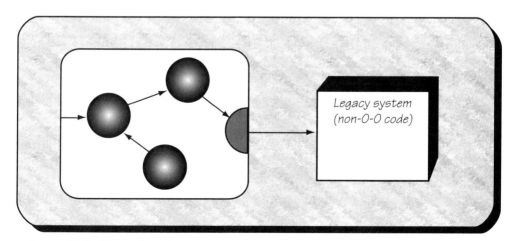

Legacy system
(non-O-O code)

Figure 5.15. Wrappering existing systems.

Objects in the system are designed to collaborate with other objects inside the O-O system. Some of these objects work with the Wrapper to deal with the legacy code.

I prefer to extend the business model slightly to hide the Wrapper from most of the current system instead of creating interfacing directly to the Wrapper. For example, if I were working in the pharmaceutical industry and we were handling dispensing for orders entered in a non–O-O order-entry system, I would instantiate and work with Orders and OrderLineItems instead of an OrderEntrySystemWrapper. The OrderEntrySystemWrapper would handle all the mechanics of interfacing to the legacy system. I would hide the fact that an OrderEntrySystemWrapper existed from all but a few classes, in this case Order and OrderLineItem.

Sometimes you find that you will create a layer of helper classes to support the legacy system interface (see Fig. 5.16). For example, if you have a set of command formats to create for requests and interpret for replies, you may create a whole framework of CommandRecord classes.

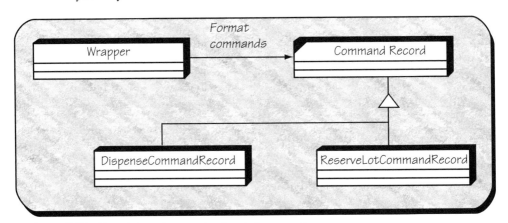

Figure 5.16. Using helper classes to interface to legacy systems.

A system object

You should have at most one system-wide global.

Systems need a way to get started. They also need a place to go for things that have no natural context (i.e., they are generally available rather than available within the context of a particular activity). These needs can be met by having one system object to be the "Grand Central Station" access router. In a pharmaceutical application, this may be the place to find open-

Orders to be filled by the system; in a real-estate underwriting application, it may be the place to find the **applications** for mortgage insurance that are waiting to be approved or denied. (See Fig. 5.17.)

The system object may be named after the project, such as **Advanced-RetailSystem**, or some object in the domain may be able to play this role, such as the **Store** in the retail domain.

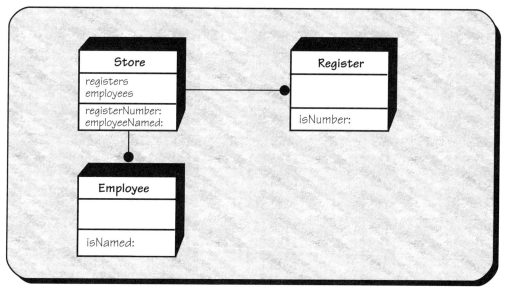

Figure 5.17. Retail industry **Store** as the system global.

The system object provides access to major objects in the business domain. In the case of the **Store**, it provides access to **Registers** and **Employees**, as shown in Figure 5.18.

```
Store
employeeNamed: aString
        "return anEmployee with name aString, else nil"
    ( self employees ) do: [ :each |
        ( each isNamed: aString ) ifTrue: [^each ].  "found"
        ].
    ^nil  "not found"
```

Figure 5.18. Example of using the system object to access employees.

An alternative to using a system-wide global in the Smalltalk dictionary is to pass the system object around to the objects that need access to it. The latter also allows multiple instances of the system to be running in a single image at the same time. Usually, the system is added as a parameter at the end of method selectors. For example, I might create a window with an **openOn:for:** method instead of just **openOn:**, as shown in Figure 5.19.

```
SalesWindow
openOn: aSalesTransaction for: aStore

    self currentObject: aSalesTransaction.
    self system: aStore.
    ...
    self open.
```

Figure 5.19. Example of passing the system object as a parameter.

Converters

This pattern is composed of sets of classes that work together to support mixed math expressions, converting the base of the values as needed.

Two idioms for this pattern deal with:

♦ **Quantity.** Expressions between different units of measure are facilitated, such as Volume, Weight, Each, and Length.

♦ **Currency.** Expressions among different monies from around the world are handled.

Let's take a closer look at the Currency idiom.

An Amount contains a value, which is a Float, and a Currency, which is an instance of one of the subclasses of Currency (Fig. 5.20). Amounts support mathematical expressions, working with their associated Currencies. They do this by using their exchangeRate to convert themselves to a common base, returning a new Amount object as the result (Fig. 5.21).

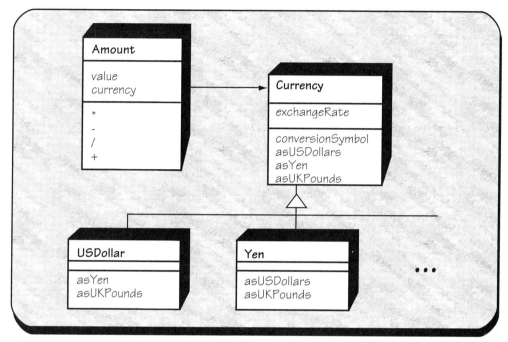

Figure 5.20. A currency exchange converter.

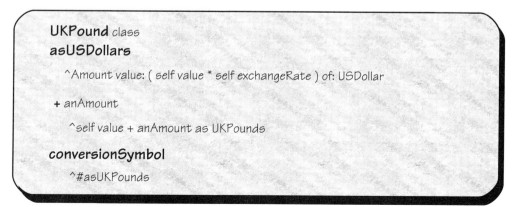

Figure 5.21. Implementing the currency exchange converter.

IPC

The Interprocess Communication (IPC) pattern uses **Proxy** objects to route messages to the real objects, which are located outside the current image (see Fig. 5.22).

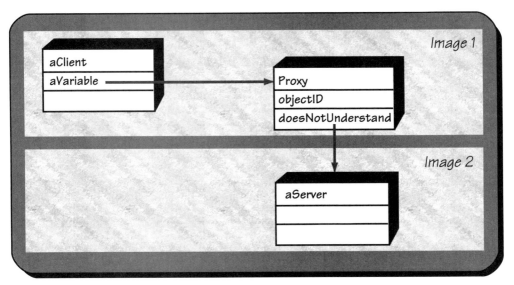

Figure 5.22. Using proxy objects between images.

One idiom uses the **Object** persistence pattern's **Registrar** to provide the access to the real object in the target image.

Enhancing reuse

Documenting contracts

As we've discussed, one way to increase the likelihood of someone reusing a component is to document it well. But you don't want to just document it in general, you want to document its *contracts*, or public interfaces.

If we look at the collaboration diagrams or the class documentation output in this book, we see a definite focus on the contractual relationships between subsystems and classes. I would strongly advise you to keep this key part of all your documentation.

Creating smaller components

In general, smaller components are more reusable, since they do fewer things and are therefore more likely to satisfy the needs of new clients without including extra unneeded functionality. There is always a trade-off between objects that can play more roles and are therefore more complex and those that are simpler and single-minded of purpose. The former are used when we know we will require the roles to be played by the same conceptual object (although **Role** objects can be explicitly defined). The latter are used in all other cases, since they are simpler to build and maintain.

Fewer, "lower" instance variables

There is some evidence that reuse is enhanced by having fewer instance variables and having them in classes that are "lower" (more deeply nested) in the inheritance hierarchy.

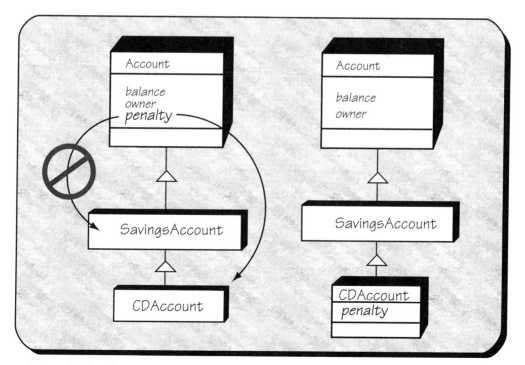

Figure 5.23. Refactoring instance variables.

For example, if we put a penalty percentage as an instance variable in Account, it would be less reusable since it doesn't stick to generic responsibilities (Fig. 5.23). Not all types of accounts can use this variable, nor do they want to inherit it. Moving this variable down to a level where accounts that incur penalties can reuse it makes the Account class itself more reusable.

I guess one way to think of this issue is to think about something you tried to reuse in the past. If it did only what you wanted or even less than what you wanted, but you wanted the functionality it did as a whole, you were probably more likely to reuse it. If it did things you did not want, you were probably less likely to reuse it.

Encapsulate pools

Ewing (1994) talks about the pitfalls of using pool dictionaries in your system. She presents the argument that more reuse can be gained by using constant-handling classes instead of simple-minded dictionaries of data. The argument is difficult to resist if you believe in a behavior-based approach to O-O development, as I do. I'll leave it to you to read her individual arguments, which I won't repeat here. I will, however, pass on the advice that you should encapsulate your constants into self-managing entities instead of lobotomized data collections.

Create abstractions

Pull the "common essence" of a group of similar types of objects into abstract superclasses. One of the key benefits of object technology is inheritance, and one of the key benefits of inheritance is leveraging abstract superclasses' methods and state data. These abstractions form as sort of mini-framework.

Let's take a look at some examples. Let's say we have an Account class that has some subclasses (see Fig. 5.24). In the Account class, we define some common behaviors as follows.

The withdraw: and deposit: methods contain logic that is generally inherited by its subclasses. The bankCode and typeString methods are empty templates that are part of the framework of being a type of Account in this design. All subclasses must define those methods. The withdraw: and de-

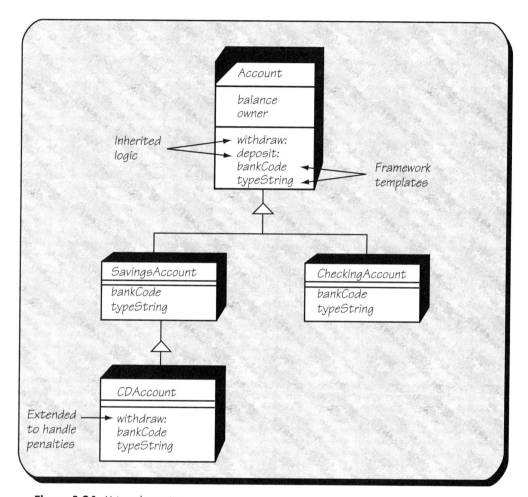

Figure 5.24. Using abstractions.

posit: methods expect these to return valid objects. View objects may use these methods also.

The CDAccount overrode the **withdraw:** method, since CDs incur a penalty for early withdrawals. The **CDAccount>>withdraw:** method should invoke the superclass' **withdraw:** method, extending it with penalty handling. This reduces the future maintenance costs.

How did we know we needed an **Account** class? The abstraction would come about one of a number of ways:

♦ **Pulling out redundant behaviors and state.** Once we have Savings-Account and CheckingAccount classes, we might notice that we have repeated some of the methods and state data. We then create an Account class as a common superclass.

♦ **Postulating an abstraction framework.** We might recognize the need for an Account class up front, creating the class and a set of required behaviors and state for any subclasses.

♦ **Reusing existing componentry.** Another project may have created some classes that apply to your project's business domain. Account might be one of these classes.

Abstractions are a key way to leverage inheritance in your designs. They facilitate reuse, organize class structures, and force you to really think about the essence of the differences in your model objects. You should have 10 to 15% abstract classes. Ewing (1993) lists a set of key characteristics of an abstract class:

♦ **It is cohesive.** All behavior is related to a few services.

♦ **It is small.** There is enough to be useful, but not too much to understand easily.[‡]

♦ **It has (little or) no state.** The design determines the details of how they collaborate with other complex objects or what simple state data is kept locally.

♦ **Default implementations are provided.** Most subclasses will inherit the logic, normally only adding some specializing methods.

[‡]I also believe that larger components are more difficult to reuse (either through delegation or subclassing) because they are more likely to include more functionality than is desired by the developer.

Ewing (1993) recognized that "any state provided by an abstract class limits subclasses, since they inherit specification of the state." There is a belief among long-term O-O developers that less state data lower in the hierarchy is better for reuse.

Use standards

There are a number of proposed or existing standards in the software industry, many of which have tools and componentry to support them. They fall into a variety of categories:

◆ **User interface.** Common User Access (CUA) from IBM is an example. Widgets that support this standard, such as notebooks and sliders, can be bought. There are also guidelines for your product's interface that can be tailored to the specifics of your situation, rather than starting from scratch.

There are some basic choices to make for a UI. At the top level, you should decide on Single Document Interface (SDI) or Multi-Document Interface (MDI). SDI matches the O-O paradigm of working with objects, so that's what I would recommend you use.

◆ **Compound document.** There are proposals for embedding complex objects within documents. Use a standard and not an ad hoc mechanism of your own.

◆ **CASE data.** There is a proposed standard for the interchange of CASE tool data called CASE Data Interchange Format (CDIF). If you build a tool, use the standard format. If you buy a tool, insist on import/export capabilities to/from CDIF.

◆ **CORBA.** The Object Management Group (OMG) has worked with a consortium of industry O-O companies to define a distributed object architecture called the Common Object Request Broker

Architecture (CORBA). Use this standard for your work with distributed objects.

Use off-the-shelf componentry

This componentry comes in many forms:

- **Icons.** IBM Icons is a catalog of hundreds of reusable icons of various types and sizes.

- **Palette-enabled components.** VisualAge has the Object Connection and encourages companies to build additional components for the palette. Visual Smalltalk has a similar program called PARTS partners.

- **Design patterns.** Gamma (1994) has reusable design patterns that you can include in your work rather than reinventing them again.

- **Use cases and scripts.** These analysis and design assets are reusable components. Embedded scripts are used in every application I've modeled. Jacobson (1992) details how to reuse use cases.

- **Classes and subsystems.** This is the (relatively) easy part. Smalltalk comes with numerous classes, and O-O development at its core is about reusing what others have built in your "reuse library" (image).

Example reusable components

Currency converter

This group of classes provides support for mixed-math arithmetic expressions for different types of currencies.

To use this compound component, all you need do is use **Amounts** instead of **Floats** and write math expressions as you normally would (Fig. 5.25).

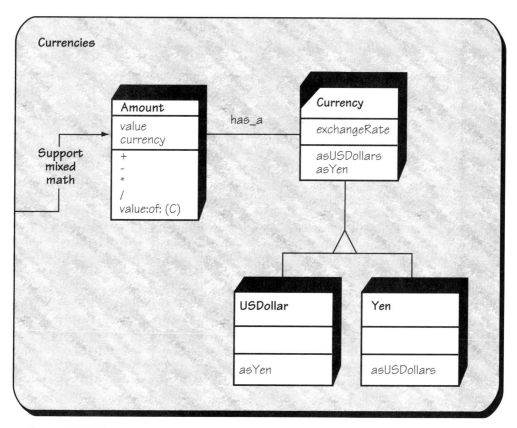

Figure 5.25. Currencies subsystem.

Documentation subsystem

As an example, I will discuss some features of a documentation subsystem that can be reused across multiple applications. In fact, this component has been reused in many Hatteras Software products.

The component is made up of multiple collaborating classes, which provide general documentation capabilities, such as using user-defined layouts to output Rich Text Format (RTF).

As the collaboration diagram in Figure 5.26 shows, a client system that uses the documentation system must support the indicated contracts:

♦ Provide formatted output

♦ Provide documentable objects

♦ Provide filtered objects

Each of these contracts consists of one or more responsibilities that will be used by the documentation system to work with the client system. The reason for these contracts is to allow the client system to control the types of objects that can be included in a document and how they are presented to the user.

To use the documentation facilities, you must write the following methods:

♦ **Provide formatted output.** The method in this contract is

→ **outputTo:** aStream **using:** aTagDictionary **for:** aDocument **nestingLevel:** anInteger **layout:** aLayout

Output myself using standard tags to aStream, according to aLayout.

♦ **Provide documentable objects.** The method in this contract is

→ **documentedModelObjects**

Return an OrderedCollection of the classes of model objects that are candidates to include as atomic units in output documentation (RTF or SGML).

♦ **Provide filtered objects.** The method in this contract is

→ **allObjectsOfType:** aString **wildCard:** aPattern

Return an OrderedCollection of all objects that are of type aString whose names (or other characteristics of your choosing) match aPattern.

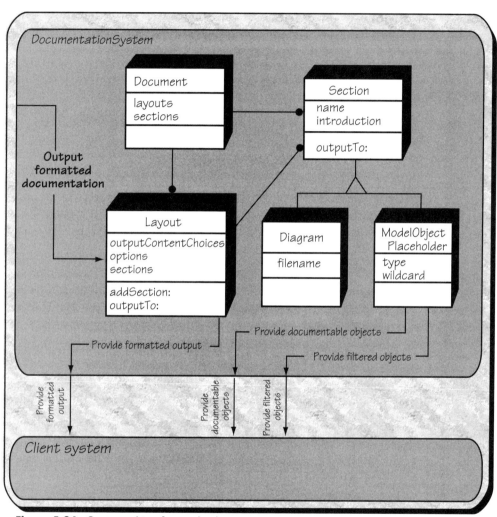

Figure 5.26. Contractual interface to the documentation system.

More portability

Use of pool dictionaries

Pool dictionaries can be used to remove platform-specific references from your code and replace them with more generic ones. The Smalltalk vendors are improving their handling of this topic, and, in fact, ParcPlace has already solved it, since portability is their forte.

For example, Smalltalk/V has a pool dictionary called PMConstants for OS/2 and WinConstants for Windows. We have defined a VConstants pool dictionary to use on both platforms which removed us one level from the naming differences.

Naming conventions

Names are very important, leading to an understandable model of your business.

I can't emphasize enough that the names you choose will affect how well your team conceptualizes the business domain objects. This will affect the quality of the design and the speed of discussions and decisions. That may sound like an exaggeration, but I firmly believe it. People can adjust to anything, but we're talking in this book about how to speed things up. Well-chosen names will help people learn the system faster and make better choices when it comes to distributing behavior, which is one of the most important tasks you will have. It is not a waste of time to hear discussions on your project like:

> *The name HistoricalEvent is more meaningful than Transaction, because we use a Transaction to represent current activities in the Store and this is dealing with an old activity for reporting purposes only.*

> *It doesn't make sense to me that an Order should be responsible for depleting Inventory. The OrderLine is related to the Item being sold and has the Quantity. Lets have the OrderLine ask the Item to deplete itself when we complete a sale.*

Class names

It is important that you avoid collisions between projects as well as off-the-shelf componentry when you define your classes. This is necessary because the Smalltalk vendors don't allow multiple name spaces, so you must simulate it yourself through conventions. The accepted de facto standard is to prefix your classes with a three-letter acronym. For example, some of the prefixes we use at Hatteras Software are (see Fig. 5.27):

- *Bas* for changes to the base image classes

- *Hat* for generic Hatteras classes

- *Doc* for classes that are part of the reusable DocumentationSystem

- *Mtx* for classes that are part of our OOMetric product

- *Hom* for classes that are part of our HOMSuite product

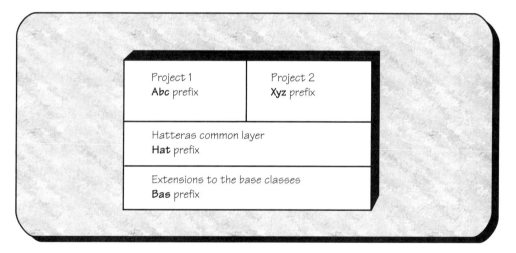

Figure 5.27. Categorizing classes using prefixes.

What you need to watch out for are classes from different groups in your company that are really the same thing. For example, if you have a project with an "Abc" prefix and another with an "Xyz" prefix that both define Order classes, someone needs to recognize that AbcOrder and XyzOrder should be merged and maintained by an independent group.

Generally, projects use one overall prefix for all classes, or they use different prefixes that relate to the subsystem the class is in.

Method names

You should pay attention to the "established" names of base and reuse library classes for the methods you create. For example, printString means something to the Smalltalk environment as well as other developers.

Chapter 6

Development tips

Making your code more robust

I'm always pleased with myself when an instance of a class of mine survives some strange new situation, possibly leaving the new reuser with a look of amazement on his face. You can almost hear "how did it do that?" in the look on his face. So, how do I do that? This section is from the school of hard knocks—lessons learned over the years that will help you as much as they've helped me.

Collection Protection

This section is about how to more safely use accessing methods. In other words, how do I maintain some semblance of encapsulation in an environment that lets me do whatever I want to (including shooting myself in the foot).

Accessing methods

The pros

There has been much debate over the years about the use of accessing methods for object-state data. I have changed my opinion over the years about the balance of the pros and cons, finally landing on the pro side. I decided to use accessing methods in most situations for the following reasons:

- ♦ **Robustness of the system under development.** Accessing methods allow me to use laissez faire initialization (often referred to as *lazy* initialization). This makes my objects more resilient, since state data (instance or class variables) initialize themselves as needed. True, an initialize message at creation can handle this situation, but then I have a maintenance problem if I forget to change the initialize method when I create new state data.

- ♦ **Facilitation of business rules and access control.** System requirements may include actions that must take place when object states change. These include security restrictions that may make the state data unavailable in certain circumstances. Accessing methods can handle these types of requirements.

- ♦ **Less coupling.** Changes to state data storage formats should not affect the class' methods and its subclasses' methods. Accessing methods remove this dependency.

If I ever run into a situation where I need to directly refer to state data, such as for performance reasons, it is easy enough to bypass the accessing methods, taking care to make sure I handle the side effects that may occur due to the above points.

I do understand the concern that blindly providing and using accessing methods negates some of the encapsulation benefits of O-O systems. I think the correct way to solve this is for the Smalltalk vendors to support one of the best capabilities of C++: the specification of *public, private,* and *protected* state data and methods. In the meantime, you do have to watch the use of another object's state data and ask yourself if you really need to get at the data, or if what you're doing should be a responsibility of the object that owns the state data. If the latter is the case, create a new public service in the owning class and request the service instead of the state data. This is not only a better design for you, but it enhances the owning class for everyone else.

The cons

One of the designs that has come back to bite me when I don't pay enough attention to what I'm doing is when I provide accessing methods to an object's state data, allowing clients to affect something they shouldn't. For example, let's say we have a RestaurantItem class and that aRestaurantItem can have condiments associated with it. We might model this situation as shown in Figure 6.1:

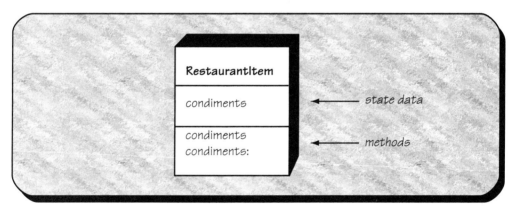

Figure 6.1. The original restaurant item.

The accessing methods would look like Figure 6.2:

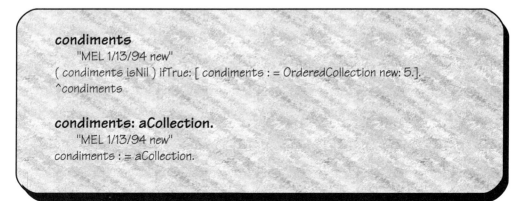

Figure 6.2. Unprotected accessing methods example.

A couple of things to note in the above code:

◆ The getting accessing method uses laissez faire initialization to create a new OrderedCollection when a client requests the uninitialized condiments for a RestaurantItem.

◆ The size of the condiments collection is explicitly specified. You certainly don't have to do this, but I have found it useful. Specifying the size forces me to think about what I'm dealing with as well as documenting the system better (i.e., a future reader now knows something more about condiments). It also saves space for small collections and execution time for large collections. Since I know that a RestaurantItem cannot have more than five condiments, I set the collection size accordingly, saving space. If I were dealing with the total collection of items in my inventory, I would use an initial size that was larger than the default, minimizing the collection creation and copying that takes place each time the collection fills up.

So, let's take a look at what happens in the client code in Figure 6.3:

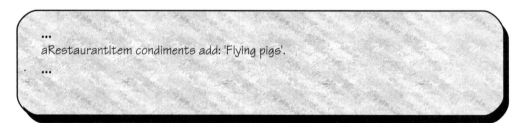

Figure 6.3. Poorly designed client code example.

Our client object just added something rather tasteless to our condiments!

An answer

So, how do we get the benefits of accessing methods without opening ourselves up to this kind of abuse? One answer is a technique that Bob Brodd came up with for use in our designs at Hatteras Software that we call *collection protection*, even though it applies to more than just collections, since collections seem to receive the most abuse. This section explains how it works and why it helps with the trade-offs discussed above.

The technique uses "public" and "private" accessing methods. These methods provide the benefits of accessing methods, without the risk caused by breaking encapsulation. Of course, there is a cost. In this case, we'll incur some additional execution-time overhead.

Protect your classes' state data from their clients' bugs.

Take a look at Figure 6.4:

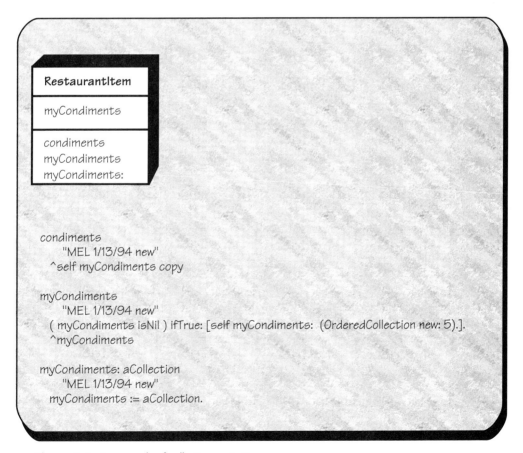

Figure 6.4. An example of collection protection.

There are some key points to this technique:

♦ The private accessing method selectors begin with the word *my* (or some other meaningful word) and return the official state data. The owning class' methods access the state data through these methods.

♦ The public accessing method selector matches the state data name and returns *a copy* of the state data. Client classes' methods access the state data information through this method.

♦ There is no public setting accessing method. Clients must use methods such as **addCondiment:** to affect the **RestaurantItem**'s condiments.

This technique means that clients do not get the real condiments *container* and thus cannot change the **RestaurantItem**'s collection of condiments. The real **Condiments** are in the copy of the collection though, so they can be changed (e.g., to change their names).

Of course, we can automate the creation of public and private accessing methods in much the same way that most groups have automated the creation of regular accessing methods.

Conclusions

The use of the state data protection mechanism described here retains the benefits of accessing methods while minimizing their drawbacks. This technique does not keep the clients' code from invoking the "private" methods, since they are not truly private, but it will normally keep unintended changes to other objects' state data from occurring.

Laissez faire initialization

Laissez faire initialization in accessing methods provides more robustness.

Laissez faire initialization[*] is a mouthful that boils down to writing instance variable accessing methods so that they self-initialize in an

---

[*]You may have heard this referred to as "lazy initialization." That's the version that's evolved by those who never had French in school. They refer to the same technique.

intelligent fashion when necessary. An example will illustrate some points (Fig. 6.5):

```
customers
"return my current customers"
( customers isNil ) ifTrue: [ self customers: ( OrderedCollection new: 50 ).].
^customers
```

Figure 6.5. An example of laissez faire initialization.

- ◆ Robustness is increased, since clients are assured that they get a well-behaved collection back (although it may be empty). The instance variable is *nil* until I need to use it.

- ◆ Dependent objects are notified of the change from the one (setting) accessing method. Note that I called my own **customer:** method instead of setting the value directly. This allows any update notification (or other actions) to take place in one set of code.

- ◆ Efficiency and self-documentation is increased by using **new:** instead of new. Collection classes will generally grow for me, but this incurs overhead in time and space (additionally causing more frequent garbage collection). By spending a few seconds to think about the expected collection size, I have added to the system documentation and reduced the execution time.

- ◆ Subclassing is easier, since I don't have to remember as many design details.

Note that the getting-accessing method uses the setting accessing method instead of directly assigning a value. This makes sure that any events that are supposed to happen whenever the value is set occur, even when it is self-initialized.

Laissez faire initialization results in objects that are more self-managing, which is good. It also can result in hiding problems in the design, which is bad. For example, perhaps anInventoryItem is always supposed to have one or more Suppliers. If we use laissez faire initialization, we may not detect the fact that the suppliers variable was initialized to an empty collection. This points out the fact that this technique should not be used blindly in all cases. Self-initialize in cases that make sense for your business, allowing the others to return *nil* if there is a bug in the system.

See the section on collection protection for techniques to use in conjunction with laissez faire initialization to ensure more robustness of your system.

Instance creation initialization

When an instance should always have certain states in order to exist, these should be set as part of creating an instance of the object. In Figure 6.6, the for: class method is used to set up aClientAccount for aClient. The business rule is that aClientAccount cannot exist without aClient.

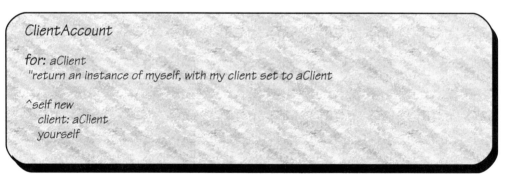

Figure 6.6. Robust instance creation example.

Instantiate through your own class methods

Most instances are created through the standard new method, which sets up the structure but not the state of the instance. This leaves a window in time when the model object is in an undesirable state and leaves it up to each client object to ensure that the model "setup" is finished properly. Both are risky.

There are several ways to handle this situation in a more robust way while easing the job for your clients, which is always desirable. The goal is to ensure that any model class instances that are created are properly set up according to your business model. This means that any state values and essential relationships with other domain objects are set up automatically.

Overriding new

You may want to write your own **new** class method, as shown in Figure 6.7:

```
Account class
new
    "force my initialization whenever I am created"

^super new initialize; yourself
```

Figure 6.7. Overriding new.

The instance receives an **initialize** message immediately and automatically upon instantiation. The **yourself** message ensures that the client receives back **anAccount** instead of whatever **initialize** returns, which is rather important!

This technique does not handle domain relationship setup well (see below for a technique that does), but it does a fine job of setting up any other state you may need. An alternative to this approach is laissez faire initialization, which is discussed elsewhere in this book.

Domain-specific instantiation methods

Many domain model objects have container relationships with other domain objects they need to communicate with in the running system.

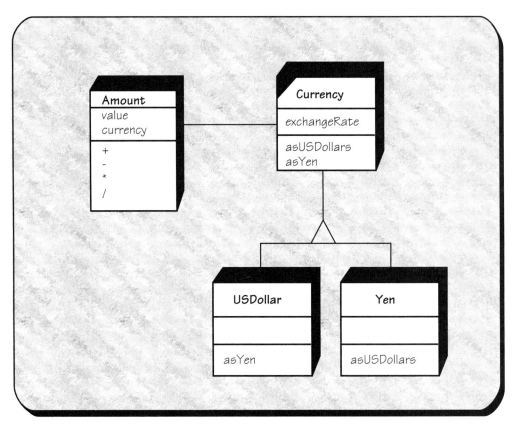

Figure 6.8. Currency conversion has_a relationship.

Let's assume that **anAmount** should never exist without **aCurrency** (Fig. 6.8). If we just use the **new** method to create **anAmount**, we will not have **aCurrency** associated with it. Certainly, we can self-initialize when we first need to work with a **Currency** object, but this is not a simple choice—which of the 30+ **Currency** subclasses do I use? (I show only **USDollar** and **Yen** above.)

A solution for this situation, which occurs fairly often in most systems, is to use custom instantiation methods for your domain model. For the

Currency example, we might create a class method called value:of: in the Amount class (Fig. 6.9).

```
Amount
value: aFloat of: aCurrencyClass
    "return a ready-to-run instance of myself with
        my value set to aFloat and
        my currency set to aCurrencyClass"

    ^self new
        value: aFloat;
        currency: aCurrencyClass;
        yourself
```

Figure 6.9. Domain-specific instantiation example.

If clients use the value:of: class method for creating new Amounts, no Amounts in the running system will be in an invalid state. If you want to force the issue even further, you could override new as in Figure 6.10:

```
Amount
new
        "force clients to use my custom instantiation methods"

        ^self error: 'You should use value:of: to instantiate Amounts'
```

Figure 6.10. Forcing use of custom instantiation methods.

If you use this technique, you need to change your custom instantiation methods to say **super** new instead of self new or else you'll invoke your own error walkback!

Using this technique helps ensure that your model cannot get into an invalid state and makes your clients' job easier.

Follow the law of Demeter

The law of Demeter[†] deals with good and bad coupling between classes. Bad coupling, which violates this law, results in more brittle designs and correspondingly higher maintenance costs.

The law states that you may only send messages to:

♦ An object passed as an argument to you

♦ An object you create

♦ self

♦ super

♦ Your class

This rules out using globals and objects returned from service requests.

```
newClient: aClient
    "add aClient to my clients"

| newAccount |
( aClient isPreferred )                  "OK, since passed as a parameter to me"
    ifTrue: [ aClient whatever ].
newAccount := ClientAccount for: aClient.
newAccount open.                         "OK, since I created it"
self checkStatus: newAccount.   "OK, since I can talk to myself"
newAccount statements
    at: self currentMonth        "NOT OK - I have no business knowing that
    put: Statement new.              newAccount keeps statements in a Dictionary"
```

Figure 6.11. Law of Demeter example.

The code in Figure 6.11 shows examples of what is allowed and not allowed. The reason the at:put: message is bad coupling is that we are dealing with implementation details of the design of the **Account** class. If this design implementation changes, this code in another class will break. This is due to the fact that we have broken encapsulation.

[†]This law of software engineering is discussed in Sakkinen (1988).

Performance

In general, you want to ignore performance during the early phases of the development effort, focusing instead on the quality of the model. However, there comes a time when performance becomes a necessary constraint on your system. You should expect performance issues to crop up according to the following frequency:

- ◆ **Model.** The least common incidence of performance problems. If you have performance problems here, you should redesign the offending portion of your system. For example, if you work with Sorted-Collections or very large Dictionaries, you can degrade performance.

- ◆ **GUI.** A fairly common performance problem area. For example, products that show large numbers of objects in icon representations within a folder on the desktop can easily perform poorly.

- ◆ **Database.** A very common performance problem area. Often, performance problems are due to a relational database (RDB) that needs tuning. For example, a schema that results in many joins to create domain objects that span multiple tables will perform poorly.

Speeding up the system

Dumb objects

There are cases where you have large collections of persistent objects. In these cases, you can use domain "dumb" objects like Strings to work with until you narrow your search.

For example, if you have 10,000 Clients for your Company, you may want to fill a selection listbox with 100 Strings for the Client names at any one time. Once a particular String is selected and an action taken, you can then instantiate aClient.

Cached objects

In the case of a large collection of objects, you can also cache some objects in memory based on a grouping such as a Category.

For example, if you have 30,000 Items in a GroceryStore, you can instantiate one Category at a time based on the last-used Item. A Category example is "peas."

System minimization

This tip correlates to the requirements management section, but this tip addresses design decisions. System minimization means that you deliver systems that contain only essential classes. This may sound obvious, but let me give you examples of ways that projects bloat their volume of classes to develop and maintain for the next two decades.

Class context

Don't create new classes based only on an object's context.

In modeling systems, projects are often tempted to create classes for situations in which the context of an object will do nicely. These situations can usually be correlated to states of the objects and can be found on state transition diagrams, if they exist.

For example, if you have Transactions that can be suspended, you can design this so that the Store holds Transactions in this state in an instance

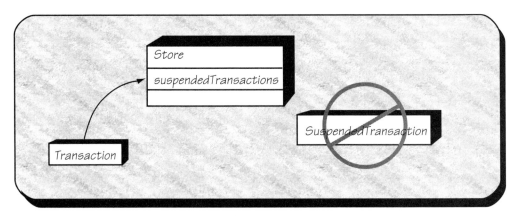

Figure 6.12. Using object context in lieu of another class.

variable called suspendedTransactions (see Fig. 6.12). This is a much better solution than to have a SuspendedTransaction class.

Make sure that the classes you define have real meaning in your domain, rather than as defined by their current state. You don't need more classes to develop and maintain.

Use roles

Roles can add flexibility to your model and design while simplifying its complexity.

For example, the same Person may be able to be a Manager, a Customer, and a SalesClerk at different times. This can be handled by allowing the Person to have multiple Roles (see Fig. 6.13).

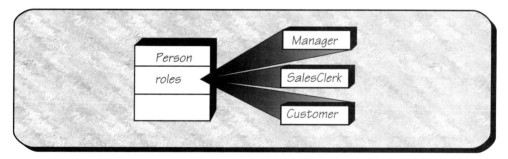

Figure 6.13. Using roles.

The Person object collaborates with its Role objects, which handle the different behaviors in different situations, such as authorizations.

This is the type of example that is often used to argue for multiple inheritance. Actually, the use of Roles more closely models the real world. When I leave my office and go home, I take on a new Role, but I am still the same Person! Also, think of the complexity as this situation continues: I am a father and a husband and a writer and a…. When do we consider multiple inheritance untenable?! (Hint: always.)

Prototype beyond the expected boundaries

A technique discussed elsewhere in this book to ensure that you don't make strategic mistakes while dealing with tactical issues is to model broadly and implement subsystems within that overall model. Another way to look at this is that you should plan to replace existing systems in a piecemeal fashion, one subsystem at a time. Either way, you will be developing, testing, and installing a portion of the overall business model. It is very difficult to clearly delineate the boundaries of your partial O-O automation. My advice is to implement slightly beyond the boundaries you perceive, using intelligent stubs at those fringes, as shown in Figure 6.14.

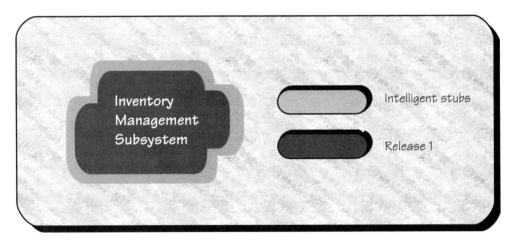

Figure 6.14. Using intelligent stubs.

So, what are intelligent stubs? They are objects and services that are beyond the perceived boundaries of the current release that contain some intelligence about how to behave. They may:

♦ **Return a hard-coded default value.** For example, you want to be able to ask a SalesClerk for its limit on the amount of change given out during one SalesTransaction. The stub could merely return $50.

♦ **Figure out what to answer from a set of possibilities.** An easy example is a "random" choice (e.g., based on milliseconds since midnight) of a set of possibilities to simulate different responses.

♦ **Return an empty, self-initialized object.** We've talked about this in the section on laissez faire initialization.

♦ **Return a simplified value.** For example, you want to be able to ask a SupplierSchedule for an optimumDeliveryDate. In the stub, you could just return the first delivery found after today's date, as shown in Figure 6.15.

Product

bestSupplier
"Return the first Supplier as a STUB.
For release 2, return the cheapest Supplier.
For release 3, include delivery schedule as a concern."
^self suppliers at: 1

Figure 6.15. Intelligent stub example.

It is difficult during O-O system development to be very clear about where the system boundaries are. The boundaries may run partially through a single class of objects (i.e., some methods are in release 1.0, some are in 2.0, and so on). If you build somewhat beyond what's expected, you won't get caught as often during function and integration testing with errors caused by hitting the developmental boundary.

Subsystem stubs

Smart stubs become even more important to consider on large projects, where you want to be able to have relatively independent groups work in parallel. The stubs would be created for the contractual interfaces between the subsystems.

The teams that have the dependencies on other subsystem(s) are responsible for developing a stub to use during the period when they do not have the real subsystem objects to talk to (Fig. 6.16). They must adhere to the architected and documented interface specifications for the stubs to ensure there are few downstream problems when the real interfaces are supported.

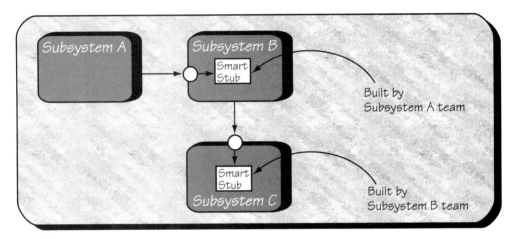

Figure 6.16. Intersubsystem stubs.

Event notification

Smalltalk has a built-in dependency mechanism that allows objects to register their interest in changes to other objects. This mechanism relies on the objects being changed to notify any registered dependents. This is a very flexible way to loosely couple the objects without hard-coding the relationship.

For example, suppose we want to update a series of views whenever some state data of an object changes. In an InventoryManagement application, the data on the screen might include numbers of Products in stock. Sales clerks taking orders over the phone want the latest quantity shown. The appropriate user interface (UI) classes would register their dependency for the Products they are showing and would receive notification if the quantity changed while the sales clerks were viewing them.

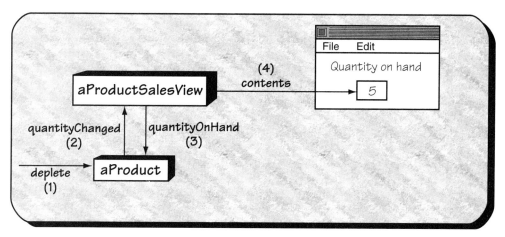

Figure 6.17. Example sequence of events for a model-view dependency update.

ParcPlace uses this dependency mechanism more effectively between model objects and views, as shown in Figures 6.17 and 6.19. Digitalk uses this mechanism only within a view, such as between panes, even though they provide some selectors for more global updates (Fig. 6.18).

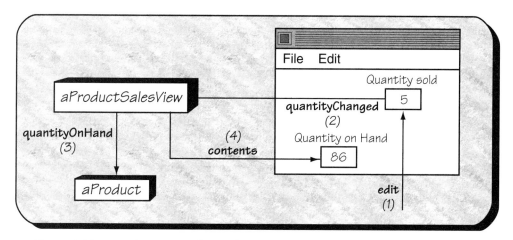

Figure 6.18. Example sequence of events for a view-view dependency update.

```
Product
deplete: anAmount
    "subtract anAmount from my amountOnHand"

  ^self amountOnHand: self amountOnHand - anAmount

amountOnHand: anAmount

  amountOnHand := anAmount.
  self changed: #amountOnHand.

ProductSalesView
initWindow

  self dependsOn: myProduct.
  ...

amountOnHand: aPane
    "myProduct's amountOnHand changed - update my view"

  self updateProductInformation.
```

Figure 6.19. Example code for handling model-view dependencies.

Code for view updating is similar, but it all takes place within the view class. Generally, some method is associated with an event, such as an add button being pushed causing a listbox to update.

Error handling

Most Smalltalk products come with some built-in error handling. What I will cover here is what you might want to include for your runtime errors.

The code in Figure 6.20 will put the stack contents from a walkback that occurs while your product is in production into a file for you. When the user calls, you can then ask her to send you the file as e-mail, along with a description of what she was doing at the time. This will help in your search for the problem.

```
Object>>runTimeError: aString
    "Capture runtime errors, dumping the stack to a user-specified file."

| aFileStream fileName |
MessageBox
    notify: 'YourApplicationName Runtime error'
    withText: 'An error was detected. Information',
            ' concerning this error will be appended to a dump file.',
            ' Please review the header section of this file for further',
            ' instructions after you have saved it.' .

fileName := (FileDialog new
        title: ( 'Append dump information to' );
        fileSpec: ( File fileName: 'Xyz_Dump' extension: 'OUT' );
        addFilter: '*.hom' description: 'Your appl name (*.XYZ)';
        addFilter: '*.*' description: 'All files (*.*)';
        save) file.
( fileName isNil ) ifTrue: [ ^self ].

(File exists: fileName)
    ifTrue: [aFileStream := File pathName: fileName.]
    ifFalse: [
        aFileStream := File pathName: fileName.
        aFileStream
        nextPutAll: '
This file contains information concerning errors detected
during the execution of YourApplName. Please give this information
along with a description of the error (including severity)
to your YourApplName coordinator or send it to internet
address: YourAddress.com
'. ].
aFileStream
    setToEnd; cr;
    nextPutAll: '######### YourApplName ERROR DUMP: #########'; cr;
    nextPutAll: Date dateAndTimeNow printString; cr;cr;
    nextPutAll: aString;cr;cr.

( MySystem loading ) ifTrue: [
        Process
        queueWalkback: aString
        makeUserIF: CurrentProcess isUserIF
        resumable: false
    ]
    ifFalse: [ Process copyStack walkbackOn: aFileStream maxLevels: 20 ].

aFileStream close.
^self
```

Figure 6.20. Example code to dump runtime walkbacks in Smalltalk/V Windows.

Design style

The way you design your O-O systems can affect the speed of delivery by allowing what I call *stealthy bugs* to creep into your system. My friend Bob Brodd and I often discuss these types of issues to come up with design guidelines for our product development at Hatteras.

Stealthy bugs

Hidden duplicates

Sets "automagically" remove any duplicates that may exist in a group of objects. This is sometimes used in defensive programming such as

```
targetAccounts asSet asOrderedCollection
```

This ensures that any targetAccounts that have been included in the grouping are not duplicates. The problem is that if this is used as a blanket design policy, bugs may be hidden. If duplicates should not happen, how did a duplicate get in the collection to begin with? These kinds of stealthy bugs can come back to haunt you later, causing problems during system testing, for example.

Hidden missing keys

Don't be too quick in how you handle possible errors— deferred problems are more difficult to diagnose.

A common protocol for the often-used Dictionary class is at:ifAbsent:, which returns an existing entry or allows the developer to take action when the entry does not exist. The default action of at: is to cause an error when a missing entry access is attempted. Specifying a block of code when encountering a missing entry is a powerful capability of the class. Problems can arise however if the actions, or lack of action, taken mask a problem. For example, the following is often seen:

```
accounts at: customerID ifAbsent: [ ]
```

Shouldn't something happen if an account for this customerID doesn't exist? What will probably happen is some later event will assume an account, which won't be there. As a minimum, the class should log a problem.

The model integrity technique alleviates this particular example by making sure that required model object relationships exist at all times. This is possible by using custom class methods to instantiate objects with their relationships immediately established. See the appendix for an example.

Scrubbing your product code

When you are finished developing a product, you should check for certain things to clean up the delivered system:

- ◆ **Self halt.** Debug statements are often inserted at various points in code under development. Search for senders of halt to make sure these are all removed.

- ◆ **References to Transcript.** The runtime system does not have a Transcript. Any code that puts out debug or other messages to the Transcript need to be removed.

Existing system wrappers

Make smart decisions about the order in which to roll out new O-O systems. For example, I recently worked with a large pharmaceutical company where they wanted a "thin slice" of functionality to be done as their pilot O-O project. It sounded good, but I found out in the first day's discussion that we were very dependent upon multiple non–O-O systems' data to drive the part we were to develop in Smalltalk. In fact, it turned out that the thin slice was very thin, since all but a handful of objects were really in the other subsystems, which we weren't supposed to be working on! But the overall system to be developed in a short period of time was now much larger, since it had to deal with at least three different subsystems (see Fig. 6.21).

Wrappering and incrementally replacing legacy systems is a good strategy, but do it along boundaries of sources of objects rather than seemingly simple functional slices.

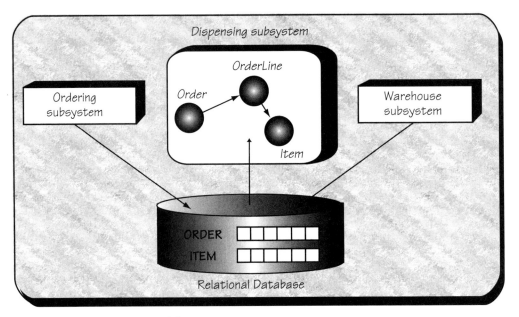

Figure 6.21. Integrating with legacy systems.

What would have been much better would be to have developed one of the other subsystems first, since they were originators of information. We could then incrementally replace the legacy system's functionality with an O-O system, "wrappering" the remaining non–O-O pieces (see the section of this book on patterns).

Documentation

Work at mentoring your own people. Everyone has areas they can improve. One easy way to help improve your people is documentation. You should document:

 ♦ **Coding guidelines.** You will spend a lot of time reading code when you develop O-O systems. Essentially, everything you do in Smalltalk is reuse. You cannot write a line of code without requesting a service from another object. Making it easier for everyone to read your code will pay off. Many Smalltalk environments now allow you to reformat methods with the click of a button.

♦ **Typical bugs and their prevention.** Johnson (1993) lists some bugs that have been repeatedly found on Smalltalk projects. These are worth studying. It is valuable to teach your people better designs to avoid these bugs in the first place. By systematically documenting them, you will shorten the learning curve for your new Smalltalk developers.

♦ **Reusable components.** As I have stated, O-O design and implementation centers around reuse. To reuse, you must be able to find components that will satisfy your requirements. Documenting your reusable components‡ will help promote their reuse.

♦ **Patterns.** Modeling patterns are high-level reusable components that can be leveraged at analysis time.

Proxy objects

Coordinate across distributed systems by using proxy objects. This technique is discussed in the section on reusing patterns.

Use code snippets

We generally keep a workspace open on a file of frequently used pieces of code.§ As a minimum, you can keep logic to initialize and run your product

---

‡*Every* project should identify and contribute some reusable components.

§The Transcript window can be used for this purpose, but if you use it be sure to save the information in a file since the Transcript contents will be lost if you crash.

under development. You can also keep code to clean up your image, such as Notifier reinitialize and FileHandle cleanHandles.

You can also use snippets of code to check out ideas and try things out. I often design and debug complex pieces of logic in a spare text pane or workspace. Smalltalk allows many areas to be used in this way. Where the complexity deserves it, I include example code as a comment at the bottom of a method.

We have developed a toolkit browser to perform many of these frequent actions for our developers. Whether you get that fancy or not, having these pieces of code around for everyone to use increases productivity.

Keep a consistently messy desk

This one seems like a nit, but I've seen many people on projects I've consulted with spend a lot of their time searching for windows they've closed or occluded with other windows. Generally, even with a VGA screen it is possible to position frequently used windows so that you can quickly get to information you need during development. I keep these windows in the same places on my desktop, overlaying each other but never completely occluded.

I also keep certain types of windows open on my desktop. For example, if I'm working in Envy™, I keep Applications Browsers open rather than a browser for a single application, since it allows easier movement between applications and has more functions on the menus. In Team/V™, I keep Package Browsers open on my model and view as well as one extra for "looking around the image."

Persistence

When you do get to the point of needing object persistence, use an object database (ODB) if you are creating a new database. This will save time in the long run. Stick to your domain, which probably isn't developing database management systems.

If you have an existing database and can't use an ODB, create a datastore layer between your model objects and your database, as discussed in the design pattern section of this book.

Smalltalk coding tips

The following collection of Smalltalk coding tips should save you some development time. Although each item is relatively small, the cumulative gain makes them worth discussing.

- ♦ **Block variables.** Use *each* as the name of your block variables so pieces of code can more easily be copied for white box reuse. Specific names are less reusable.

- ♦ **Spell words out.** Your abbreviation may be perfectly clear to you, but it's not to other people! Keep in mind that everyone spends a lot of time reading code in an O-O system.

- ♦ **Prefix class names with a three-letter acronym.** This alleviates name collisions. For example, we used *Inv* for the Inventory Management application.

- ♦ **Use accessor methods.** Name them the same as the instance variables they reference.

- ♦ **Use "my" for private collection accessing.** Answer a copy of the collection as a public service. For example, the method my-Customers is used internally by InvCompany; the method customers returns a copy of the collection, making the model class more robust.

♦ **SortedCollection.** Don't keep SortedCollections around—they don't perform well. Sort collections only when you need to, such as for view listboxes, and convert them to something else. For example,

> self customers: self customers asSortedCollection asOrderedCollection.

Method names

It is important that you follow established conventions when naming methods. This is one time when you should probably bow to established names, rather than use your own choice. You can always create "synonym" methods by your name to do the same thing. Established names can be found in areas of the system like the Collection classes. Method names such as at: and first should be used if you are created a container object of your own.

Unfortunately, the "established" names are not explicitly listed somewhere you can go and look them up. They have evolved as meaningful, descriptive names used in many applications and/or included in the base classes. Your company should plan on including the names from your domains and/or conventions in documentation that your O-O projects can use. Also note that frameworks define de facto standard names for subclasses and client classes.

I recommend that you try to name methods so that your code will read well. One technique that helps readability is to leave off get and set on accessing method names.

For example,

> myAccount balance

reads better than

> myAccount getBalance

Variable names

One technique I recommend for variable names is to use plural forms when a collection is kept. I also recommend generally keeping the implementation choice out of the name. For example, I would use

> products

rather than

> productArray

Crisp descriptions

Similar to the importance of names, clearly describing the classes in your system and their contractual behaviors is essential to the rapid development of a solid object model. My rule of thumb is that I write a short description of every class and subsystem I create when I create it. If you can't crisply describe an object, something is wrong and you should keep discussing that area of the domain until it is clear. In my opinion, it is a mistake to continue before everyone is clear on what the new object is. This fosters the conceptual model in everyone's head, which is important to the effective development of your system.

Clear descriptions are important, especially for your key classes and contracts.

Testing

One of the areas least dealt with in the industry today is O-O testing. While working at IBM, I worked on some tools to support O-O testing, including how to effectively deal with the issues of coverage, reusable test cases, and inheritance as they related to testing for Smalltalk. Some of what I learned is in Lorenz (1993). I will discuss some more advice in this section.

Use case-driven

Use cases are excellent inputs for writing function and system test plans and test cases, since they focus on the major functionality of the system. They are not suitable for unit testing (see Intelligent clustering, below).

Intelligent clustering

You will write a lot of test code. In fact, Rettig (1991) predicts that you will write twice as much test code as production code! So, how can you minimize the time and effort required to deliver a high-quality product? Some advice:

Group classes based on coupling for testing purposes.

- ◆ **Group classes into meaningful clusters.** This will make it easier to set up testbeds. Look for clusters for testing in similar ways you look for subsystem boundaries—based on the amount of coupling. In Figure 6.22, it will probably be easiest to test **Class1** and **Class2** together and before **Class3** and **Class4**, which should also be tested together. Lorenz (1993) discusses at some length the process of building upon previously certified classes.

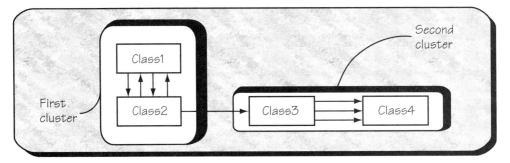

Figure 6.22. Example of clustering by coupling.

Class1 and **Class2** interact heavily to service their contracts. Similarly, **Class3** relies heavily on **Class4** to get its work done. It is not efficient to test them separately.

We can build upon a certified foundation if we cluster starting with our lowest-level, most localized sets of classes and build upwards to more wide-reaching classes within our domain (Fig. 6.23).

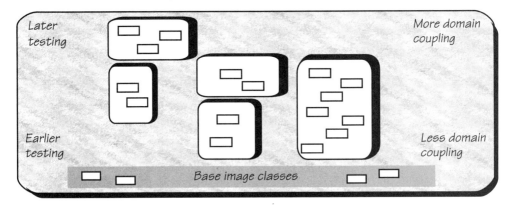

Figure 6.23. Bottom-up testing strategy.

So how does clustering save effort? Let's take a look at an example. Let's say that I have a requirement to handle conversions between weights. I create classes as shown in Figure 6.24:

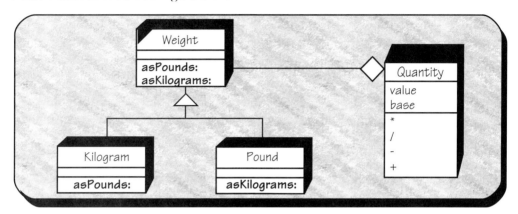

Figure 6.24. Looking at object coupling for cluster testing.

The Weight classes provide the conversion table functionality. The Quantity class uses the Weight classes to manipulate its value to allow math between values of different Weight types. Client objects can now use mathematical expressions such as (10 lbs * 5 kg).

Now let's look at testing these classes. Let's say I want to test the Quantity class by itself. I would have to provide the functionality of the Weight classes in my testbed code, since I am not using the actual classes.

You could argue that I could test the Weight classes and then use them to test the Quantity class, and you'd be right. The question is whether this is added value or not worthy of the extra effort required. Also, this is a simple example and many clusterings will have more complications for setting up testbeds for smaller groupings or individual classes.

Public protocol focus

When testing an O-O system, focus your effort on the public methods of the class clusters. If these are robust and meet their requirements, you have proven that the cluster is solid for its public interface.

The primary focus of testing should be on the public methods.

You can use the Smalltalk environment to make sure no one is invoking the private methods. Reporting could easily be automated based on method selectors. Testing of private methods, all possible paths, and coverage are nice possible tests to run that will help you clean up unused code. The question is of course whether this (possibly large) effort results in a good return on the investment. On projects I run, the answer is "no."

Regression testing

The following changes affect previously run tests:

+ **New classes inserted in the middle of the hierarchy.** In this case, you have to look at what behaviors are affected by the change. In Figure 6.25, the deplete: method must be retested for all subclasses of ItemForSale.

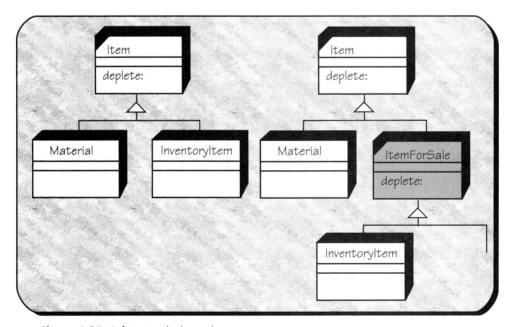

Figure 6.25. Refactoring the hierarchy.

♦ **Method edits.** In this case, changing the **deposit**: method in the Account class will require retesting the behaviors related to deposits in all of its subclasses (Fig. 6.26).

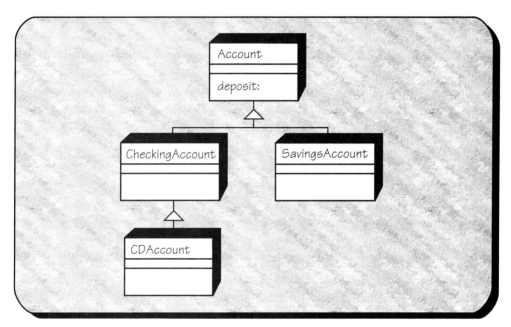

Figure 6.26. Inherited methods.

Chapter 7

Conclusions

The world is moving so fast these days that the man who says it can't
be done is generally interrupted by someone doing it.

—Elbert Hubbard

IN THIS BOOK, we've covered a lot of ground geared toward helping you develop quality software using object technology more quickly than you have before. We have discussed a number of ways you can do this, including:

♦ **Reuse.** This is the number one way you can speed up your development cycle, but you must be willing to make the upfront investment to make it happen.

Modeling and design patterns and frameworks give you the biggest return on your investment. A reuse process will grow your reuse library for reduced cycle times on future projects.

♦ **Education.** Mentoring, formal training, and bringing in consultants are all forms of education for your people.

Reuse is the number one means to achieve rapid software development.

◆ **An iterative process.** Controlling the iterations through estimates, schedules, and staffing geared toward an iterative process will reduce risk.

◆ **Focusing on behavior.** A methodology that focuses your efforts on behavior first and foremost will result in an object model that will serve your company's needs for many years to come.

◆ **Design techniques.** Laissez faire initialization, collection protection, avoiding stealthy bugs, and other techniques make for a more robust system.

◆ **Design metrics.** The law of Demeter, method overrides, inheritance hierarchy nesting level, method complexity, class size, and method size measurements will focus your design reviews on the highest return in increased quality.

If I've succeeded in helping you in even one or two of the areas covered in the book, that's great. Perhaps you can revisit some other areas when the time is right to see if they are more applicable to your situation. Good luck, take care, and keep in touch.

Appendix

Inventory Management sample application

T HIS APPLICATION IS an intentional oversimplification of a real application, in order to quickly move through an O-O development cycle. I have included an annotated recounting of the progress of portions of the application using the methodology presented in this book as an expanded example.

This section follows an actual group working through a portion of the application development, starting with an imprecise set of requirements and finishing with a functional prototype of a portion of the application. The group was made up primarily of novices to O-O development. We met for half-day sessions at a time. This was a mentored workshop and the steps and work done closely matches an actual project. We did simplify the problem in some areas, like pricing, which can be whole projects themselves.

Group dynamics

My strategy in mentoring groups is to get them doing the work themselves very quickly. We ran the project in our apprentice center. This gets us away from the regular day-to-day interruptions and surrounds us with a variety of the best tools and O-O people available.

During each session, I or another O-O mentor initially sat at HOM-Suite™, Visio™, Smalltalk, and WindowBuilder™ entering the information as we discussed the use case, scenarios, model choices, and design techniques. Within a couple of hours of starting each new task, I would ask another member of the team to "sit in the hotseat." This forces the team members to learn the tools as well as be more active in the process and decisions. Even quiet people must speak up in this situation.

Initial requirements statement

As is usually the case on a real project, the requirements are imprecise and need to be clarified and verified through writing use cases and scenario scripts. The following requirements were the only inputs given to the team. An end user was available to answer questions.

1. Users must be able to call in and give us their name, address, and phone number to be put on our mailing list.

2. Sales reps must be able to take orders over the phone. The orders will include quantity and customer information.

3. The system should allow browsing by name, keyword out of the description, and item number of the inventory items. Quantities will be kept on items.

4. When items are sold, the inventory stock should be changed accordingly. Tax calculation, shipping orders, and bill printing will occur as orders are taken.

5. Orders will be logged. The log will include an indication of the source of the order (e.g., magazine ad or coupon in the mailer).

6. Items will be reordered automatically once a minimum level has been reached. Multiple suppliers are possible for an item.

7. Inventory and sales reports will be possible.

Day 1

Today's goal was to get a solid start on an object model. We are focusing on the public behaviors, largely ignoring the private behaviors and state data for now. We wrote a use case and started building an object model by two techniques:

♦ **Parts of speech.** We examined the use case, which is a requirements analysis document, and looked at the nouns to find candidate classes.

We listed a number of classes, stopping at each one and describing it crisply and succinctly. This resulted in our finding a number of abstractions along the way, such as Form and Role. We also found some synonyms, such as Item and Product.

Once we found a number of classes, we organized them into a set of subsystems. We looked for functionally related portions of the business to define our initial subsystems. We assigned contracts to the main subsystems, Sales, Shipping, and Stocking.

♦ **Scenario script writing.** We started the most basic script possible for our domain, identifying alternative script paths along the way. We filled in model details as we went, rapidly switching between the model browser and the script browser.

Some issues were raised and noted as we went. Many would have been resolved in a more timely fashion on a real project, since they were more global decisions than we could easily bypass in reality. This was a necessary trade-off for the compressed lifecycle.

We had a discussion about whether an Order was a formatted report or whether it was an active Transaction. We decided it was active and renamed it OrderTransaction.

There was confusion about the different states of an OrderTransaction, so we drew a state transition diagram (Fig. A.1).

Normally, we don't need very many state transition diagrams, and I expect this to be the only one we draw.

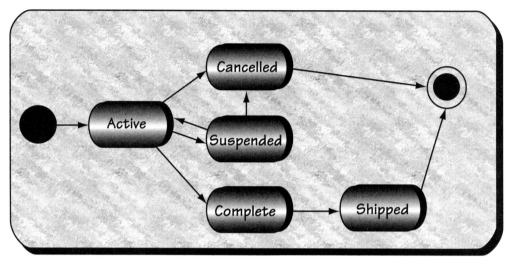

Figure A.1. OrderTransaction state transition diagram.

Basic mail-order sale
Assumptions:
  Orders only. Not dealing with complaints, problems, returns yet.
  This order is for an existing customer.
  Information is current since no automatic depletion and reordering is handled yet.
  No product attributes can be entered, such as size and color.
  Item numbers are entered for products, instead of types of products.
  This customer has good credit and no credit limit.
  We only ship one way.

The salesperson answers the phone and asks the customer for her phone number.
The customer's information appears on the screen and the salesperson verifies the name and address.

The salesperson asks the customer for an item number. The salesperson sees the item information and verifies the type of product being requested. The salesperson asks for a quantity and enters it.
The salesperson asks for more item numbers until the customer is done ordering.

The salesperson verifies the last credit card used or gets new credit card information.
The salesperson tells the customer the total amount and when to expect the shipment.

The inventory is updated once the order is committed by the customer. The invoice and picking slip are printed in the warehouse. The picker collects the items and puts them in a box for the shipment. He includes the picking slip in the box and puts the invoice on the outside as a shipping label. Once the shipment is completely satisfied, the order is archived. Until then, the order is outstanding. The picker takes the shipment to the shipping dock for pickup.

Figure A.2. The first use case.

Use cases

We wrote one use case, focusing on the primary usage of the system (Fig. A.2). In this case, it was receiving an order over the phone from an existing customer.

Scenario scripts

We started writing a scenario script, filling in the object model details as we went (Fig. A.3).

A convention that I follow is to capitalize the names of classes in the text of scripts.

> **Basic mail-order sale**
> This script details our phone order-taking procedures from customers
> **InterfaceSubsystem** requests customerFor: aPhoneNumber from **Company**
>   **Company** asks hasPhoneNumber: aPhoneNumber from **Person**
>   **script:** New customer
>   **script:** Customer information updates
>   **branch:** Bad credit record
> **InterfaceSubsystem** requests productNumbered: aNumber from **Inventory**

Figure A.3. The first day's partial scenario script.

We realized that we needed a **Company** object when we went to find our Customer (**aPerson**) by her phone number. We then immediately added the **customerFor:** responsibility to the **Company** class, since we used it in the script. Similarly, we created a **hasPhoneNumber:** responsibility for **Person** (which is playing the role of our customer) and **productNumbered:** responsibility for **Inventory**.

Classes

The following classes were entered into HOMSuite™ as we went through our analysis techniques and discussions. We focused on discovering the key classes. This set already includes many of the classes that are essential to an inventory management application.

We focused initially on the major contracts between the key classes and subsystems. We were trying to get a foundation for the architecture of the system.

For this application, the key classes include Product, Inventory, Order-Transaction, LineItem, and Shipment. They are key because they are central to the business domain. It would be difficult to imagine building this application without them.

We primarily named the classes, described what they represent in our model, identified contracts, and identified a few public responsibilities based on the script-writing. Toward the end of the day we grouped the classes into subsystems.

A key class, essential to this business domain.

Company
Our business is "The Hatteras Electronics Boutique"

Owner	nil
Subsystem	System
Superclass	Object (A)
Subclasses	

"*" = a public method that has not been assigned to a contract yet.

Public responsibilities
*customerFor: aPhoneNumber
Return aCustomer, based on aPhoneNumber
Instance state data
customers
My customers

CustomerRole
The Person that initiates an Order.

Owner	nil
Subsystem	Sales
Superclass	Role (A)
Subclasses	

(A) = an abstract class.

Form (A)
A format for information, used to display, print, etc.

Owner	nil
Subsystem	Reporting
Superclass	Object (A)
Subclasses	Invoice (I) PickingSlip

A key class, essential to this business domain.

Inventory
A collection of Products that we sell.

Owner	nil
Subsystem	Stocking
Superclass	Object (A)
Subclasses	

Public responsibilities
*productNumbered:
aNumber

Return the Product with number aNumber,
else nil

Invoice (I)

A printed bill containing a Customer's address, Product information from the Order, total cost.

Owner	nil
Subsystem	Shipping
Superclass	Form (A)
Subclasses	

Issues
* Customer Invoices versus Supplier Invoices
We will need to handle this difference once we allow receiving.

(I) = an open issue is associated with this object.

LineItem

A quantity of a Product within an Order.

Owner	nil
Subsystem	Sales
Superclass	Object (A)
Subclasses	

Public responsibilities
*price

A key class, essential to this business domain.

Object (A)

Owner	nil
Subsystem	System
Superclass	nil
Subclasses	Company Form (A) Inventory LineItem Person Product Role (A) Shipment(I) Transaction(A) Warehouse

OrderTransaction

A Transaction between the Customer and the Company.

Owner	nil
Subsystem	Sales
Superclass	Transaction (A)
Subclasses	

Contracts and associated Responsibilities
Move Items from Inventory to the Customer
Public responsibilities
*shippingCost
*tax
*total

A key class, essential to this business domain.

Person

Owner	nil
Subsystem	System
Superclass	Object (A)
Subclasses	

Public responsibilities
*hasPhoneNumber:
aPhoneNumber
Answer a boolean indicating whether my phoneNumber is aPhone-
Number.

PickerRole
The Person that fills Shipments based on PickingSlip contents.

Owner	nil
Subsystem	Shipping
Superclass	Role (A)
Subclasses	

PickingSlip
A printout listing Products, Product locations in the Warehouse, amounts, Order number, Picker.

Owner	nil
Subsystem	Shipping
Superclass	Form (A)
Subclasses	

A key class, essential to this business domain.

Product
An Item in the Inventory that a Customer can order.

Owner	nil
Subsystem	Stocking
Superclass	Object (A)
Subclasses	

Contracts and associated Responsibilities
Maintain inventory levels
Public responsibilities
*price
Instance state data
number

Role (A)

Owner	nil
Subsystem	System
Superclass	Object (A)
Subclasses	CustomerRole PickerRole SalespersonRole

SalespersonRole
A Person who takes Orders from Customers.

Owner	nil
Subsystem	Sales
Superclass	Role (A)
Subclasses	

Shipment (I)

A container with the Products for one Order for a Customer.

Owner	nil
Subsystem	Shipping
Superclass	Object (A)
Subclasses	

A key class, essential to this business domain.

Issues

* Supplier Shipment versus Customer Shipment
    We need to handle both once we can handle receiving.

Transaction (A)

An active object that handles an external event.

Owner	nil
Subsystem	System
Superclass	Object (A)
Subclasses	OrderTransaction

Warehouse

The storage area where Products are kept and available for packing to fulfill Orders.

Owner	nil
Subsystem	Warehousing
Superclass	Object (A)
Subclasses	

Day 2

Today's goals were to get through the main scenario for our first use case, draw a collaboration diagram, and continue filling in details in the object model. Most of today was spent creating responsibilities and not many new classes. We know that we have other unexplored areas of the business domain, such as the activities in the Warehouse, that will focus on a different set of classes.

Collaboration diagram

We drew collaboration diagrams after the rapid modeling session ended for the day, using our extended RDD palette for Visio (see Fig. A.4).

This diagram helped us conceptually grasp the important relationships of our business domain. We mixed collaborations (uses), shown with arrows, and associations (has_a) between classes and subsystems.

We showed every subsystem-level contract that we had identified at this time. We showed every key class as well as important public responsibilities of the key classes.

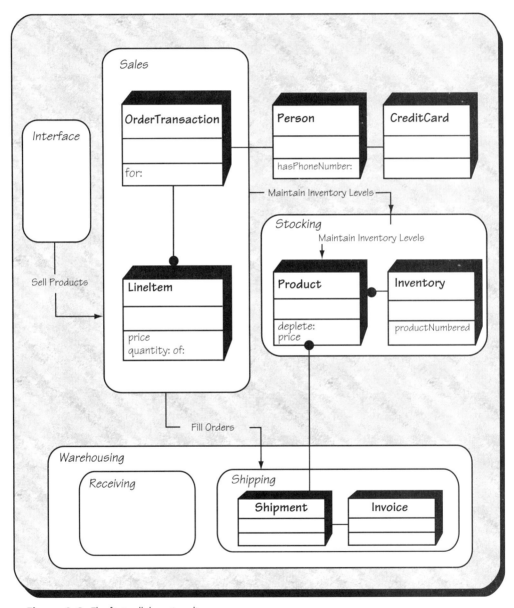

Figure A.4. The first collaboration diagram.

Model integrity

An important modeling state choice made was to use class methods to instantiate instances that immediately have their key model relationships established. I call this technique "instantiation integrity."

For example, the LineItem>>quantity:of: class method returns an instance of a LineItem with its quantity and Product states set (Fig. A.5).

You should build your model classes so that they cannot accidentally be in a bad state, according to your business rules.

```
LineItem class
quantity: aNumber of: aProduct
    "return an instance of myself with my quantity set to aNumber and
    my product set to aProduct"

    ^self new
        quantity: aNumber;
        product: aProduct;
        yourself
```

Figure A.5. Model state robustness through custom class method instantiation.

We viewed the fact that a LineItem should not exist without an associated Product as an important business rule.

OrderTransaction>>for: is a class method that works similarly to ensure that we don't allow OrderTransactions to exist without an associated customer (a Person).

Scenario script

We finished the first script through the ordering process (Fig. A.6). We still have to handle the activities in the warehouse as well as explore the additional scripts we have identified.

Basic mail-order sale
- This script details our phone order-taking procedures from customers
InterfaceSubsystem requests customerFor: aPhoneNumber from **Company**
    Company asks hasPhoneNumber: aPhoneNumber from **Person**
        script: New customer
        script: Customer information updates
        branch: Bad credit record
InterfaceSubsystem sends for: aPerson to **OrderTransaction**
- Iterate across the following steps for each product the customer orders.
InterfaceSubsystem requests productNumbered: aNumber from **Inventory**
    Inventory asks isProductNumber: aNumber for each **Product**
        script: Product not found
InterfaceSubsystem asks name, description, and price from **Product**
InterfaceSubsystem sends sellQuantity: aNumber of: aProduct to **OrderTransaction**
    OrderTransaction sends quantity: aNumber of: aProduct to **LineItem**
        LineItem sends deplete: aNumber to **Product**
InterfaceSubsystem asks total from **OrderTransaction**
- End of line item sale.
InterfaceSubsystem asks creditCard from **Person**
InterfaceSubsystem asks number, expirationDate from **CreditCard**
script: New credit card
script: Out-of-stock lineItems
script: Order cancelled

Figure A.6. The completed first script.

Subsystems

We organized the classes into a number of subsystems according to the functionally related areas of the business domain.

(I)Accounting
  Owner   nil
  Issues
   * Partial accounting
    We do not really account for receivables and payables yet.
  Alternatives

Interface
  Owner   nil

Receiving
  Owner   nil

Reporting
    Owner   nil
    Classes
    Form (A)

Sales
    Owner   nil
    Contracts
      *Sell Products
    Classes
    CreditCard (A)
    CustomerRole
    LineItem
    MasterCardCreditCard
    OrderTransaction
    SalespersonRole
    VisaCreditCard

Shipping
    Owner   nil
    Contracts
      *Fill Orders
    Classes
    Invoice (I)
    PickerRole
    PickingSlip
    Shipment (I)

Stocking
    Owner   nil
    Classes
    Inventory
    Product

System
    Owner   nil
    Classes
    Company
    Object (A)
    Person
    Role (A)
    Transaction (A)

Warehousing
    Owner   nil
    Classes
    Warehouse

Classes

A few additional classes were identified today, but mostly we filled in required behaviors as we went statement by statement writing the script.

Company
Our business "The Hatteras Electronics Boutique"
Owner	nil
Subsystem	System
Superclass	Object (A)
Subclasses	
Public responsibilities	

  *customerFor:
    aPhoneNumber
    Return aCustomer, based on aPhoneNumber
Instance state data
customers
My customers

Class ownership is already coming into play.

CreditCard (A)
Owner	Lori Wynkoop
Subsystem	Sales
Superclass	Object (A)
Subclasses	MasterCardCreditCard VisaCreditCard
Public responsibilities	

  *expirationDate

  *isVisa
    Returns false as a default for all my subclasses.
  *number

CustomerRole
The Person that initiates an Order.
Owner	nil
Subsystem	Sales
Superclass	Role (A)
Subclasses	

Form (A)
A format for information, used to display, print, etc.
Owner	nil
Subsystem	Reporting
Superclass	Object (A)
Subclasses	Invoice (I) PickingSlip

Inventory
A collection of Products that we sell.

Owner	nil
Subsystem	Stocking
Superclass	Object (A)
Subclasses	

Public responsibilities

*productNumbered:
   aNumber
   Return the Product with number aNumber, else nil

Invoice (I)

A printed bill containing a Customer's address, Product information from the Order, total cost.

Owner	nil
Subsystem	Shipping
Superclass	Form (A)
Subclasses	

Issues

* Customer Invoices versus Supplier Invoices
We will need to handle this difference once we allow receiving.

Alternatives

LineItem

A quantity of a Product within an Order.

Owner	nil
Subsystem	Sales
Superclass	Object (A)
Subclasses	

Public responsibilities

*price
*quantity:of: (C)
   aNumber, aProduct
   Returns an instance of myself with quantity set to aNumber and my
   product set to aProduct.

This class method ensures that we will not have aLineItem without aProduct.

MasterCardCreditCard

Owner	Lori Wynkoop
Subsystem	Sales
Superclass	CreditCard (A)
Subclasses	

Object (A)

Owner	nil
Subsystem	System
Superclass	nil
Subclasses	Company CreditCard (A) Form (A) Inventory LineItem Person Product Role (A) Shipment (I) Transaction (A) Warehouse

OrderTransaction

A Transaction between the Customer and the Company.

Owner   nil
Subsystem   Sales
Superclass   Transaction (A)
Subclasses

Contracts and associated Responsibilities

Move Items from Inventory to the Customer

Public responsibilities

*for: (C)
    aPerson
    Return an instance of myself with my customer set to aPerson.
*sellQuantity:of:
    aNumber, aProduct
    Returns aLineItem
*shippingCost

*tax

*total

This class method ensures that we will not have anOrderTransaction without aPerson (customer).

Person

Owner   nil
Subsystem   System
Superclass   Object (A)
Subclasses
Public responsibilities

*address

*creditCard

*hasPhoneNumber:
    aPhoneNumber
    Answer a boolean indicating whether my phoneNumber is aPhone-
    Number.
*name

PickerRole

The Person that fills Shipments based on PickingSlip contents.

Owner   nil
Subsystem   Shipping
Superclass   Role (A)
Subclasses

PickingSlip

A printout listing Products, Product locations in the Warehouse, amounts, Order number, Picker.

Owner   nil
Subsystem   Shipping

Superclass Form (A)
Subclasses

Product
An Item in the Inventory that a Customer can order.
Owner nil
Subsystem Stocking
Superclass Object (A)
Subclasses
Contracts and associated Responsibilities
Maintain inventory levels
Public responsibilities
deplete:
  aNumber
  Subtract aNumber from my quantityOnHand, creating a RestockOrder
  if necessary.
*description

*isProductNumber:
  aNumber
  Returns a Boolean indicating whether a number matches my number.
*name

*price

Instance state data
number

More assignments of public responsibilities to contracts is taking place.

Role (A)
Owner nil
Subsystem System
Superclass Object (A)
Subclasses CustomerRole   PickerRole   SalespersonRole

SalespersonRole
A Person who takes Orders from Customers.
Owner nil
Subsystem Sales
Superclass Role (A)
Subclasses

Shipment (I)
A container with the Products for one Order for a Customer.
Owner nil
Subsystem Shipping
Superclass Object (A)
Subclasses
Issues
 * Supplier Shipment versus Customer Shipment

We need to handle both once we can handle receiving.
Alternatives

Transaction (A)
An active object that handles an external event.

Owner	nil
Subsystem	System
Superclass	Object (A)
Subclasses	OrderTransaction

VisaCreditCard

Owner	Lori Wynkoop
Subsystem	Sales
Superclass	CreditCard (A)
Subclasses	

Warehouse
The storage area where Products are kept and available for packing to fulfill Orders.

Owner	nil
Subsystem	Warehousing
Superclass	Object (A)
Subclasses	

Day 3

Today, we wrote additional scripts, filling in responsibilities along the way.

Scenario scripts

We explored a new area of the model, dealing with the picking and shipping of the Products for a Shipment. We also went back and filled in the details for a couple of the scripts we had identified, based upon what would result in an application with some interesting areas being functional in a short time (see Figs. A.7–A.9).

Basic mail-order sale
- This script details our phone order-taking procedures from customers
OrderWindow requests customerFor: aPhoneNumber from **Company**
    Company asks hasPhoneNumber: aPhoneNumber from **Person**
    script: New customer
    script: Customer information updates
    branch: Bad credit record
OrderWindow sends for: aPerson to **OrderTransaction**
- Iterate across the following steps for each product the customer orders.
OrderWindow requests productNumbered: aNumber from **Inventory**
    Inventory asks isProductNumber: aNumber for each **Product**
    script: Product not found
    script: Product search
OrderWindow asks name, description, and price from **Product**
OrderWindow sends sellQuantity: aNumber of: aProduct to **OrderTransaction**
    OrderTransaction sends quantity: aNumber of: aProduct to **LineItem**
        LineItem sends deplete: aNumber to **Product**
OrderWindow asks total from **OrderTransaction**
- End of line item sale.
OrderWindow asks creditCard from **Person**
OrderWindow asks number, expirationDate from **CreditCard**
script: New credit card
script: Out-of-stock lineItems
script: Order cancelled
- We're now in the Warehouse
OrderWindow requests submit to **OrderTransaction**
    OrderTransaction requests printFor: self to **Invoice**
        Invoice asks customer, total from **OrderTransaction**
        Invoice asks name, address, phoneNumber, from **Person**
        Invoice asks lineItems from **OrderTransaction**
        Invoice asks quantity, productName, unitPrice, price from **LineItem**
        Invoice requests print: self from **Printer**
script: Print picking slip
    - We're allowing the Warehouse personnel to verify that shipment is shipped
    OrderTransaction sends complete to **ShippingStatusWindow**
- Sometime later..............
        ShippingStatusWindow sends shipped to **OrderTransaction**
    OrderTransaction sends log: self to **OrderLog**
    script: Log order to disk

Figure A.7. Updated main scenario script.

New customer
- This script handles the case where an Order is received from someone
- we have not dealt with yet.
OrderWindow openOn: aCompany to **CustomerWlndow**
     CustomerWlndow requests named: aName to **Person**
     CustomerWlndow sends addCustomer: aPerson to **Company**

Figure A.8. Second scenario script..

Product search
- Searches for a product if productNumber not known by name, description.
OrderWindow sends openOn: anInventory to **ProductSearchDialog**
- Search by name
    ProductSearchDialog sends productNameMatching: aPattern to **Inventory**
       Inventory sends nameMatches: aPattern to each **Product**
    ProductSearchDialog sends openOn: aCollection to modeless
    ProductSelectionMSDialog
- Search by description
    ProductSearchDialog sends productDescriptionMatching: aPattern to **Inventory**
       Inventory sends descriptionMatches: aPattern to each **Product**
    ProductSearchDialog sends openOn: aCollection to modeless
                ProductSelectionMSDialog

Figure A.9. Third scenario script.

Collaboration diagram

We updated our collaboration diagram to show additional essential classes and key responsibilities (Fig. A.10).

We reused the **Role** design pattern to allow the same **Person** to play both a CustomerRole as well as a SalespersonRole.

Code generation

We generated Smalltalk/V™ code from HOMSuite™, setting the global class prefix to Inv to ensure we didn't have any name collisions. Since we aren't generating for Envy™ or Team/V™, the generated code does not group the classes into applications or packages, respectively.

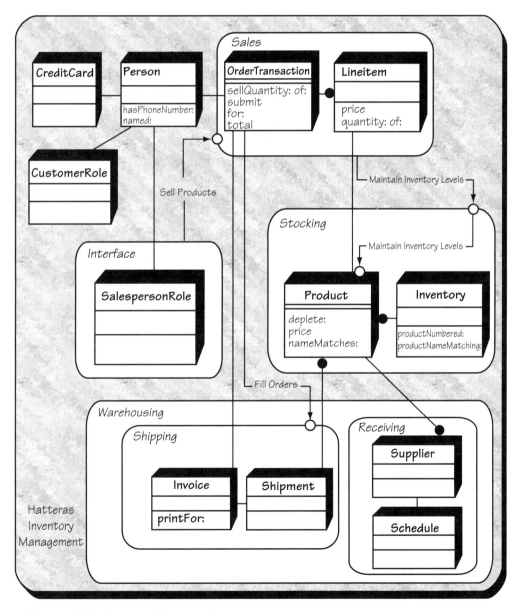

Figure A.10. Updated collaboration diagram.

```
Object subclass: #InvCompany
    instanceVariableNames:
        ' customers '
    classVariableNames: ''
    poolDictionaries: ''   !

InvCompany subclass: #InvSupplier
    instanceVariableNames: ''
    classVariableNames: ''
    poolDictionaries: ''   !

Object subclass: #InvCreditCard
    instanceVariableNames: ''
    classVariableNames: ''
    poolDictionaries: ''   !

InvCreditCard subclass: #InvMasterCardCreditCard
    instanceVariableNames: ''
    classVariableNames: ''
    poolDictionaries: ''   !

InvCreditCard subclass: #InvVisaCreditCard
    instanceVariableNames: ''
    classVariableNames: ''
    poolDictionaries: ''   !

Object subclass: #InvDevice
    instanceVariableNames: ''
    classVariableNames: ''
    poolDictionaries: ''   !

InvDevice subclass: #InvOutputDevice
    instanceVariableNames: ''
    classVariableNames: ''
    poolDictionaries: ''   !

InvOutputDevice subclass: #InvPrinter
    instanceVariableNames: ''
    classVariableNames: ''
    poolDictionaries: ''   !

Object subclass: #InvForm
    instanceVariableNames: ''
    classVariableNames: ''
    poolDictionaries: ''   !

InvForm subclass: #InvInvoice
    instanceVariableNames: ''
    classVariableNames: ''
    poolDictionaries: ''   !
```

```
InvForm subclass: #InvPickingSlip
    instanceVariableNames: ''
    classVariableNames: ''
    poolDictionaries: ''   !

Object subclass: #InvInventory
    instanceVariableNames: ''
    classVariableNames: ''
    poolDictionaries: ''   !

Object subclass: #InvLineItem
    instanceVariableNames: ''
    classVariableNames: ''
    poolDictionaries: ''   !

Object subclass: #InvLog
    instanceVariableNames: ''
    classVariableNames: ''
    poolDictionaries: ''   !

InvLog subclass: #InvOrderLog
    instanceVariableNames: ''
    classVariableNames: ''
    poolDictionaries: ''   !

Object subclass: #InvPerson
    instanceVariableNames: ''
    classVariableNames: ''
    poolDictionaries: ''   !

Object subclass: #InvProduct
    instanceVariableNames:
        ' number '
    classVariableNames: ''
    poolDictionaries: ''   !

Object subclass: #InvRole
    instanceVariableNames: ''
    classVariableNames: ''
    poolDictionaries: ''   !

InvRole subclass: #InvCustomerRole
    instanceVariableNames: ''
    classVariableNames: ''
    poolDictionaries: ''   !

InvRole subclass: #InvPickerRole
    instanceVariableNames: ''
    classVariableNames: ''
    poolDictionaries: ''   !
```

```
InvRole subclass: #InvSalespersonRole
    instanceVariableNames: ''
    classVariableNames: ''
    poolDictionaries: ''    !

Object subclass: #InvSchedule
    instanceVariableNames: ''
    classVariableNames: ''
    poolDictionaries: ''    !

Object subclass: #InvShipment
    instanceVariableNames: ''
    classVariableNames: ''
    poolDictionaries: ''    !

Object subclass: #InvTransaction
    instanceVariableNames: ''
    classVariableNames: ''
    poolDictionaries: ''    !

InvTransaction subclass: #InvOrderTransaction
    instanceVariableNames: ''
    classVariableNames: ''
    poolDictionaries: ''    !

Object subclass: #InvWarehouse
    instanceVariableNames: ''
    classVariableNames: ''
    poolDictionaries: ''    !
```

!InvCompany class methods !

classComment
          "Code generated by HOMSuite, a Hatteras Software tool on
          Dec 21, 1994."

          "-------------------------------------
          < startClass > Company
          < description > Our business ""The Hatteras Electronics Boutique""

          < subsystemName > System
              ....
              Hatteras Software, Inc.
              919.319.3816
              71214.3120@compuserve.com
          ----------------------------------" !   !

!InvCompany methods !

customerFor: aPhoneNumber

Subsystems and contracts are carried forward as commentary in vanilla Smalltalk. Envy or Team/V systems would use applications, packages, and categories that are a part of the group development environment.

"Return aCustomer, based on aPhoneNumber"
!

addCustomer: aPerson
        "adding aPerson to our customers"
!   !

!InvCreditCard class methods !

classComment
        "Code generated by HOMSuite, a Hatteras Software tool on
        Dec 21, 1994."

"-------------------------------------
< startClass > CreditCard
< description >
< subsystemName > Sales

        ....
        Hatteras Software, Inc.
        919.319.3816
        71214.3120@compuserve.com
--------------------------------" !   !

!InvCreditCard methods !

number
        ""
!

expirationDate
        ""
!

isVisa
        "Returns false as a default for all my subclasses."
!   !

!InvPrinter class methods !

classComment
        "Code generated by HOMSuite, a Hatteras Software tool on
        Dec 21, 1994."

"-------------------------------------
< startClass > Printer
< description > This is used to print out Forms, such as Invoices and PickingSlips
in the Warehouse.
< subsystemName > Interface

        ....
        Hatteras Software, Inc.

```
        919.319.3816
        71214.3120@compuserve.com
        ----------------------------------" !   !
```

!InvPrinter methods !

print: anInvoice
        "format and print out anInvoice"
!   !

!InvInvoice class methods !

classComment
        "Code generated by HOMSuite, a Hatteras Software tool on
         Dec 21, 1994."

```
    "-------------------------------------
    < startClass > Invoice
    < description > A printed bill containing a Customer's address,
    Product information from the Order, total cost.

    Invoice is a transitory thing and can be recreated
    if necessary.

    < subsystemName > Shipping
            ...................................
    Hatteras Software, Inc.
    919.319.3816
    71214.3120@compuserve.com
    ----------------------------------" !   !
```

!InvInvoice methods !

printFor: anOrderTransaction
        "Format customer and order information for anOrderTransaction
        and send to printer."
!   !

!InvInventory class methods !

classComment
        "Code generated by HOMSuite, a Hatteras Software tool on
         Dec 21, 1994."

```
    "-------------------------------------
    < startClass > Inventory
    < description > A collection of Products that we sell.
    < subsystemName > Stocking
```

```
        ....................................
        Hatteras Software, Inc.
        919.319.3816
        71214.3120@compuserve.com
        ---------------------------------" !   !
```

!InvInventory methods !

productNumbered: aNumber
    "Return the Product with number aNumber, else nil"
!

productNameMatching: aPattern
    "return any Products whose name matches aPattern"
!

productDescriptionMatching: aPattern
    "return any Products whose description matches aPattern"
!   !

!InvLineItem class methods !

classComment
      "Code generated by HOMSuite, a Hatteras Software tool on
      Dec 21, 1994."

```
    "---------------------------------------
    < startClass > LineItem
    < description > A quantity of a Product within an Order.
    < subsystemName > Sales
        ....................................
        Hatteras Software, Inc.
        919.319.3816
        71214.3120@compuserve.com
        ---------------------------------" !
```

quantity: aNumber **of:** aProduct
    "Returns an instance of myself with quantity
     set to aNumber and my product set to aProduct."
!   !

!InvLineItem methods !

price
    ""
!

quantity

Model integrity is maintained through class methods that instantiate objects with required relationships already established.

"return my quantity"
!

productName
   "return my Product's name"
!

unitPrice
   "return my Product's unit price"
!   !

!InvOrderLog class methods !

classComment
        "Code generated by HOMSuite, a Hatteras Software tool on
        Dec 21, 1994."

   "-------------------------------------
   < startClass > OrderLog
   < description > archival of OrderTransactions on disk
   < subsystemName > Shipping
        ....
        Hatteras Software, Inc.
        919.319.3816
        71214.3120@compuserve.com
   ----------------------------------" !   !

!InvOrderLog methods !

log: anOrderTransaction
        "write a formatted report to disk of OrderTransaction"
!   !

!InvPerson class methods !

classComment
        "Code generated by HOMSuite, a Hatteras Software tool on
        Dec 21, 1994."

   "-------------------------------------
   < startClass > Person
   < description >
   < subsystemName > System
        ....
        Hatteras Software, Inc.
        919.319.3816
        71214.3120@compuserve.com
   ----------------------------------" !

named: aName
""
! !

!InvPerson methods !

hasPhoneNumber: aPhoneNumber
"Answer a boolean indicating whether my phoneNumber is
aPhoneNumber."
!

name
""
!

address
""
!

creditCard
""
!

phoneNumber
"return my phoneNumber"
! !

!InvProduct class methods !

classComment
"Code generated by HOMSuite, a Hatteras Software tool on
Dec 21, 1994."

"--------------------------------------
< startClass > Product
< description > An Item in the Inventory that a Customer can order.
< subsystemName > Stocking< synonym > Item
    < startContract > Maintain inventory levels

    ....
    Hatteras Software, Inc.
    919.319.3816
    71214.3120@compuserve.com
----------------------------------" ! !

!InvProduct methods !

price
            ""
!

isProductNumber: aNumber
    "Returns a Boolean indicating whether a number matches my number."
!

name
         ""
!

description
               ""
!

deplete: aNumber
    "Subtract aNumber from my quantityOnHand,
    creating a RestockOrder if necessary."
!

nameMatches: aPattern
    "return aBoolean indicating whether my name matches aPattern"
!

descriptionMatches: aPattern
        "return aBoolean indicating whether my description matches aPattern"
!   !

!InvOrderTransaction class methods !

classComment
        "Code generated by HOMSuite, a Hatteras Software tool on
        Dec 21, 1994."

"------------------------------------
< startClass > OrderTransaction
< description > A Transaction between the Customer and the Company.

< subsystemName > Sales
< startContract > Move Items from Inventory to the Customer

    ....
    Hatteras Software, Inc.
    919.319.3816
    71214.3120@compuserve.com
---------------------------------" !

We determined that Products should be responsible for their own depletion and reordering, since this would be much more complicated to handle at the Inventory level.

for: aPerson
      "Return an instance of myself with my customer set to aPerson"
! !

!InvOrderTransaction methods !

Again, we enforce the business rule that an Order-Transaction cannot exist without a customer (aPerson) through custom class methods.

total
      """
!

tax
      """
!

shippingCost
      """
!

sellQuantity: aNumber **of:** aProduct
      "Returns aLineItem"
!

submit
      "This causes Warehousing to print an Invoice and a PickingSlip
      and mail it, etc."
!

customer
      "return my customer (aPerson)"
!

lineItems
      "return a **copy** of my LineItems (collection protection)"
! !

Development environment

The team created some sample windows in WindowBuilder Pro™ to prepare for tomorrow, when we will hook the UI to the model (Figs. A.11 and A.12).

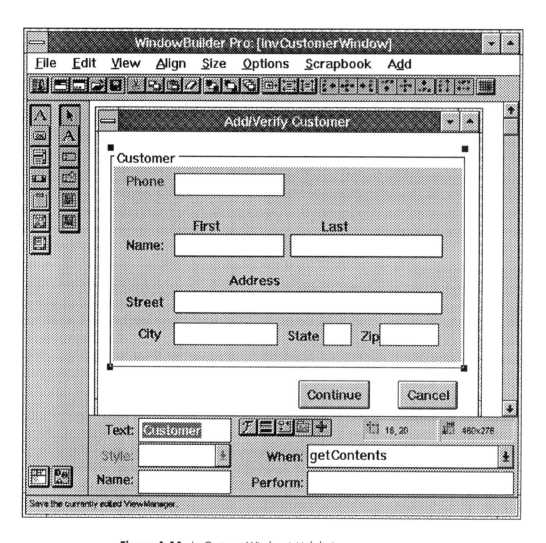

Figure A.11. InvCustomerWindow initial design.

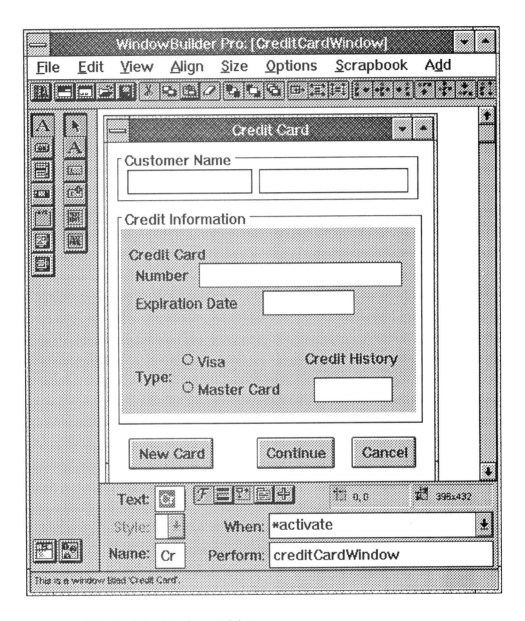

Figure A.12. CreditCardWindow initial design.

Day 4

The more you use the code under development, the more solid it becomes.

Today, we connected the UI to the model, filling in functionality as we went. We want to use the production code as much as possible, even during our very early development. The more we can use the code, the more solid it will become. So, as we incrementally add functionality and iteratively rework functionality, we are using as much of the actual system as we can.

Development environment

The focus of the method development is on using accessing methods, laissez faire initialization for the getting methods, and collection protection. We are building the most robust model classes that we can, so that clients cannot accidentally cause us to reach a bad state.

We wanted to create frameworks for both our model classes and our UI classes. We created a layer for commonality to "bubble to the top" for these two categories (see Figs. A.13 and A.14).

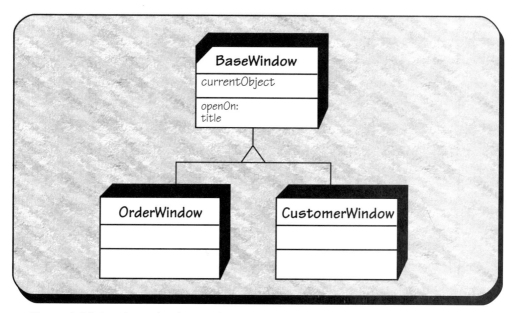

Figure A.13. Initial view class framework.

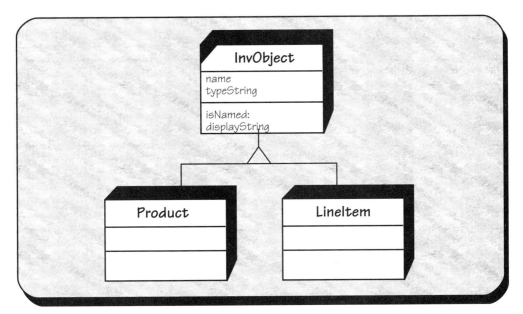

Figure A.14. Initial model class framework

Code

The following code examples show some of the techniques discussed in the book being used during our development.

```
Object subclass: #InvCompany
    instanceVariableNames:
        'name customers '
    classVariableNames: ''
    poolDictionaries: '' !
```

!InvCompany class methods !

classComment
        "Code generated by HOMSuite, a Hatteras Software tool on
        Dec 21, 1994."

    "-------------------------------------
    < startClass > Company
    < description > Our business ""The Hatteras Electronics Boutique""
    < subsystemName > System
```
```

```
....................................
Hatteras Software, Inc.
919.851.0993
71214.3120@compuserve.com
-----------------------------------"!
```

fakeCustomers
> "return aCollection of Persons to use for testing"

> ^OrderedCollection new
>   add: (InvPerson new firstName: 'Lori';
>   phoneNumber: '555-1111'; yourself);
>   add: (InvPerson new firstName: 'Denise';
>   phoneNumber: '555-2222'; yourself);
>   yourself! !

You often need to create dummy data to "prime the pump" when initially setting up your system development.

!InvCompany methods !

addCustomer: aPerson
> "adding aPerson to our customers"

> (self myCustomers includes: aPerson) ifTrue: [
>   ^MessageBox notify: 'Hatteras Inventory System'
>   withText: (aPerson name, ' already exists.')
>   ].
> ^self myCustomers add: aPerson!

Model objects should keep control of their own instance variables. Clients can request modification of the state, but not directly modify instance variables.

customerFor: aPhoneNumber
> "Return aCustomer, based on aPhoneNumber"!

customers
> " Return a **copy of our customers - collection protection.**"

> ^self myCustomers copy!

Clients get a copy of the collection, so that they cannot accidentally change the real collection's contents."

loadCustomers
> "PRIVATE for testing only!!!!"

> ^customers addAll: self class fakeCustomers!

myCustomers
> " PRIVATE Return our customers "

> (customers isNil) ifTrue: [
>   customers := OrderedCollection new: 100.
>   self loadCustomers.   "set up fake set of Persons for testing"
>   ].
> ^customers!

The real accessing method adds "my" to the front of the variable name.

name

```
( name isNil ) ifTrue: [ ^'Unnamed' ].
^name!

typeString

    ^' company'! !

ViewManager subclass: #InvBaseWindow
    instanceVariableNames:
        'currentObject '
    classVariableNames: ''
    poolDictionaries: '' !

!InvBaseWindow class methods ! !

!InvBaseWindow methods !

currentObject

    ^currentObject!

currentObject: anObject

    currentObject := anObject.!

openOn: anObject

    self currentObject: anObject.
    self labelWithoutPrefix: self title.
    self open.!

title

    ^self currentObject name, self currentObject typeString! !
```

There are a number of things you can put into a GUI framework. This code shows some of the initial methods we created for our Window classes.

Days 5 through N

Subsequent days are filled with iterations on the code, feeding back changes as needed to the model. Many of these changes were refactoring of responsibilities between classes. Over time, the changes become less and less frequent as the business model firms up through continuous validation.

This mini-project was a learning experience for all of us. It is quite possible to do a lot of good modeling and development work in a few weeks.

However, be aware that most domains have many complex areas, each of which can go relatively quickly, but as a whole generally add up to a significant investment. The payoff is downstream on future projects in the same domain.

Again, we enforce the business rule that an OrderTransaction cannot exist without a customer (aPerson) through custom class methods.

Glossary

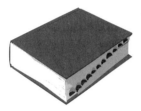

Abstract class. A class that has no instances. A class that contains common methods and state data to facilitate sharing among its subclasses.

Accessing method. A method that is used to get or set an instance variable. Accessing methods allow you to perform laissez-faire initialization. They are usually very short, almost standard, methods that are left out of some measurements.

Analysis. That part of software development concerned with modeling (part of) business.

Anthropomorphism. To attribute human qualities to something. A useful technique for understanding the dynamics of an object model.

Architect. A person with a broad view of the system's interrelationships who owns the subsystem contracts.

Black box. To ignore the internal design of something. In reuse, to collaborate through message sends without understanding the detailed workings of a design. In testing, to certify a class through exercising the public methods only. Contrast with *white box*.

Business domain. An area of focus of activities for a particular business. A problem domain. For example, retail, insurance, finance, and communications are areas in which different businesses specialize their products and services.

Business process reengineering. A set of activities geared toward defining the direction of the company's future efforts.

Class. A template that defines the structure and capabilities of an object instance. The class definition includes the state data and the behaviors for the instances of that class.

Class hierarchy. A tree structure that organizes class inheritance.

Class hierarchy nesting. The number of subclassing levels from the top in the class hierarchy.

Class cluster. A relatively small group of classes that collaborate with each other a great deal. Clustering them simplifies the amount of work required to test the functionality.

Comment line. A physical line in a method or class definition that contains a comment.

Concrete class. A class with instances in the runtime system.

Contract. A simplifying abstraction of a group of related public responsibilities that are to be provided by subsystems and classes to their clients.

Delegation. Requesting services from another object rather than performing the work yourself. The most common form of reuse.

Design. That part of software development concerned with the mapping of a business model into an implementation.

Domain. An area of knowledge or expertise. Examples are banking, insurance, telecommunications, and retail.

Dynamic model. That portion of the object model documentation that deals with the collaborations that take place in a running system, including scenario scripts.

Framework. A set of prebuilt classes and methods that define the basic structure of some end user functions, leaving the application-specific details to be filled in by developers.

A portion of a software system that is designed to provide some useful services through refinement and extension by client developers.

At an implementation level, a set of classes that cooperate to achieve the goal of providing some functionality.

An implementation of a design pattern.

Heuristic. A guideline based on trial-and-error usage. A rule of thumb.

Idiom. An example design or implementation instance that has proven useful multiple times in the past and is therefore recommended as a starting point for similar endeavors.

Incremental process. Development steps that result in piecemeal additions of new application functions over the life of the project.

Instance variable. A name that allows one object (instance) to refer to another one. The instance variables make up an object's state data.

Iteration. A single cycle of an iterative process, consisting of planning, production, and assessment phases over a multi-month period of time.

Iterative process. Development steps that result in multiple deliveries of the same application functions over the life of the project.

Key class. A class that is central to the business domain being automated. A key class is one that would cause great difficulties in developing and maintaining a system if it did not exist.

Laissez faire initialization. A technique whereby instance variables are initialized when they are needed and not beforehand. This allows for more self-managing objects and system robustness, with a cost of additional overhead.

Line item. A unit of effort on a software project, assigned to one person and developed during one iteration.

Method. A class service or behavior. Methods are executed whenever an object receives a message. They contain the logic, in the form or more message sends, for the objects in a class.

Method extension. In a subclass, to invoke the superclass' method of the same name followed by logic to extend the behavior.

Method override. To create a method in a class with the same name as a method in one of its superclasses. This results in different behavior for the same message. Template methods and method extensions are not considered overrides.

Metric. A standard of measurement. Used to judge the attributes of something being measured, such as quality or complexity, in an unbiased manner.

O-O. Object oriented.

Object model. A representation of a business domain using objects.

Pattern. A basic design rule that can be used to guide the development of frameworks.

Reuse. To use something in a new situation without modification.

Reengineer. To pull information out of a development environment and object model and selectively update your model and/or your development environment so that the two match.

Scenario script. A sequence of steps the user and system take to accomplish some task. There is a script for each of the major end-user functions provided by the system.

Specialization. An extension of the behavior of a type of object.

Static model. That portion of the business' object model documentation that deals with the fixed relationships between objects, such as *is_a inheritance and has_a container relationships.*

Stereotype. A characterization of a type of behavior of an object, such as whether the object actively drives actions in the system or passively provides information to other objects. A role an object plays in a particular situation.

Subsystem. A design abstraction that groups a set of classes that provide a related group of end user functions.

Support class. A class that is not central to the business domain being automated, but provides basic services or interface capabilities to the key classes.

Template method. A method that identifies the need for all subclasses of a class to define its behavior, but does not define a default behavior.

Use case. See *scenario script.*

White box. To examine the internal design of something. In reuse, to subclass, copy a piece of code, or some other technique requiring the understanding of the detailed workings of a design. In testing, to exercise the internal workings of a class through an understanding of its logic paths and private and public methods. Contrast with *black box*.

WOOD. Workshop on Object-Oriented Development.

References

Beck, Kent, "Patterns and Software Development," *Dr. Dobb's Journal*, no. 211, February 1994, pp. 18–22.

Beck, Kent, "To accessor or not to accessor?" *The Smalltalk Report*, vol. 2, no. 8, June 1993, pp. 8, 22.

Booch, Grady, "Designing an Application Framework," *Dr. Dobb's Journal*, no. 211, February 1994, pp. 24–32.

Boyd, Nik, "Building object-oriented frameworks," *The Smalltalk Report*, vol. 3, no. 1, September 1993, pp. 1, 4–6, 14–16.

Coplien, James O., "Pattern languages for organization and process," *Object Magazine*, July–August 1994, pp. 47–51.

Ewing, Juanita, "Abstract classes," *The Smalltalk Report*, vol. 3, no. 2, October 1993, pp. 15–16.

Ewing, Juanita, "Getting real: Constants, defaults, and reusability," *The Smalltalk Report*, vol. 2, no. 5, February 1993, pp. 13–14, 16.

Ewing, Juanita, "Pools: An attractive nuisance," *The Smalltalk Report*, vol. 3, no. 6, March–April 1994, pp. 1, 4–6.

Gamma, Erich, Richard Helm, Ralph Johnson, and John Vlissides, *Design Patterns: Elements of Object-Oriented Software Architecture*, Reading, MA: Addison-Wesley, 1994, p. 21.

Harmon, Paul, and David Taylor, *Objects in Action*, Reading, MA: Addison-Wesley, 1993.

Hendley, Greg and Eric Smith, "GUIs: GUI-based application development: some guidelines," *The Smalltalk Report*, vol. 2, no. 6, March/April 1993, pp. 16–18.

Jacobson, Ivar, Magnus Christerson, Patrik Jonsson, and Gunnar Overgaard, *Object-Oriented Software Engineering: A Use Case Driven Approach*, Reading, MA: Addison-Wesley, 1992.

Johnson, Ralph, "Classic Smalltalk bugs," *The Smalltalk Report*, vol. 2, no. 7, May 1993, pp. 5–9.

Kolbe, Kathy, *The Conative Connection*, Reading, MA: Addison-Wesley, 1990.

Lorenz, Mark, "Introducing VisualAge," *The Smalltalk Report*, vol. 4, no. 1, September 1994, pp. 14–16.

Lorenz, Mark, *Object-Oriented Software Development: A Practical Guide*, Englewood Cliffs, NJ: Prentice Hall, 1993.

Lorenz, Mark, *Object-Oriented Software Metrics: A Practical Guide*, Englewood Cliffs, NJ: Prentice Hall, 1994.

Lorenz, Mark, "Real world reuse," *Journal of Object-Oriented Programming*, November/December 1991, pp. 35–39.

Lorenz, Mark, "When the worst happens," *The Smalltalk Report*, vol. 4, no. 2, October 1994, pp. 25–26.

Love, Tom, *Object Lessons*, New York: SIGS Books, 1993.

McCabe, T. J., "A complexity measure," *IEEE Transactions on Software Engineering*, vol. 2, 1976, pp. 308–320.

Object Management Architecture Guide, Framingham, MA: Object Management Group, 1993.

Rasmus, Daniel W., "What can we learn from AI?" *Object Magazine*, February 1994, pp. 65–67.

Rettig, Marc, "Testing made palatable," *Communications of the ACM*, vol. 34, no. 5 May 1991, pp. 25–29.

Rochat, Roxie and Juanita Ewing, "Smalltalk debugging techniques," *The Smalltalk Report*, vol. 2, no. 9, July–August 1993, pp. 1, 18–23.

Sakkinen, M., "The law of demeter and C++," *SIGPLAN Notices,* vol. 23, no. 12, December 1988, pp. 38.

Sridhar, S., "Implementing peer code reviews in Smalltalk," *The Smalltalk Report,* vol. 1, no. 9, July–August 1992, pp. 1, 8–13.

Tanaka, David, "A clash of cultures?" *Computing Canada,* November 23, 1992, p. 45.

Verity, John W., and Evan I. Schwartz, "Software Made Simple," Business Week, September 30, 1991, pp. 92–100.

Wirfs-Brock, Rebecca, "Stereotyping," *Object Magazine,* Nov.–Dec. 1993, pp. 50–53.

Wirfs-Brock, Rebecca, "Characterizing Object Interactions," *Working paper at the WOOD workshop,* Snowbird, Utah, February 7–9, 1994.

Wirfs-Brock, Rebecca, "How designs differ," *Report on Object Analysis and Design,* Nov.–Dec. 1994, pp. 51–53, 56.

Wirfs-Brock, Rebecca, Brian Wilkerson, and Lauren Wiener, *Designing Object-Oriented Software,* Englewood Cliffs, NJ: Prentice Hall, 1990.

Index